ADVERTISING
FOR MODERN RETAILERS

ADVERTISING FOR MODERN RETAILERS

Making It Work in a Consumer World

Shirley F. Milton

FAIRCHILD PUBLICATIONS, INC. • NEW YORK

FIGURE AND ILLUSTRATION ACKNOWLEDGMENTS: p. 12, *Good House-keeping* Magazine; p. 56, Anne Kurz; p. 70, Jantzen Sportswear; p. 85, John Baldwin; The Tog Shop; p. 89, NBC Radio Division; National Broadcasting Company, Inc.; p. 94, Bonwit Teller; p. 125, Bergdorf Goodman; p. 126, B. Altman & Company; 300 line Frank Brothers ad inserted in the *New York Times* and the *Wall Street Journal* in May, 1972 produced by KFO, Inc. Advertising; p. 128, Franklin Simon; p. 135, Courtesy of Saks Fifth Avenue; p. 136, Wallachs Inc.; The Gorham Company; pp. 138-139, Henri Bendel; p. 142, Bograd Brothers; The Kroger Company; p. 144, Franklin Simon; p. 152, Gimbels; p. 153, Bloomingdale's; p. 174, Gimbels; p. 175, J.C. Penney; p. 177, GAR-FINCKEL's, Washington, D.C.; Georg Jensen; Lord & Taylor; Courtesy of Saks Fifth Avenue; p. 178, B. Altman & Company; Courtesy of Saks Fifth Avenue; p. 179, Fruit of the Loom, Inc.; Maurice Villency; p. 182, Field Brothers; p. 225, The Better Business Bureau of Metropolitan New York, Inc.

Standard Book Number: 87005-100-8
Library of Congress Catalog Card Number √72-97758
Manufactured in the United States of America

DEDICATED TO GABRIEL AND DAVID

CONTENTS

ACKNOWLEDGMENTS

This book has benefited from many people whom I can and will name, as well as from many more who have educated, guided, criticized, and inspired me through many years.

Those who can be singled out include my colleagues in the Department of Advertising and Communication at Fashion Institute of Technology, principally Professors Arthur Winters and Gilbert Kahn and Professor-emeritus Stanley Goodman. Acknowledgment must also be made to Walter Vetter, Vice-President of Television Bureau of Advertising; Frank Orenstein, Vice-President, Research, Bureau of Advertising, ANPA; and Seymour Helfand, Vice-President, of International Council of Shopping Centers, all of whom gave me invaluable time and source materials. NBC provided local television and radio coverage maps. Pitney-Bowes-Alpex Inc. provided up-to-the-minute information on POS, SPICE, and PEPPER, the new electronic monitors of merchandising.

Special thanks should be given to my editors, Ed Gold and Shelly Ruchlin, whose assistance made this a pleasant and rewarding task. The local offices and Research Bureau of Fairchild Publications have provided prompt and intelligent assistance.

Among those who cannot be named individually must be included many of my students whose questions and probing led to additional investigation on my part.

SHIRLEY F. MILTON
New York, July 17, 1973

INTRODUCTION

i

The need for a textbook devoted entirely to retail advertising is a real one. The need is equally great for trained, concerned personnel, skilled in this specific area. Despite the fear of computerization, the call goes out for capable men and women, and increases year by year.

Retail advertising is an area that requires man to understand man, the neighborhood storekeeper to know his customers, the downtown or branch store management to know its customer-population, and the shopping center's promotion director to understand *his* customers.

In sum, the need to understand the customer—and how to reach him—is especially strong for the retail store, which is, after all, closest to that customer.

Marketing, as a skill and an area of business, is on everyone's tongue, but *retail marketing* is a stepchild. Relegated to the back chapters of book after book—and there given only partial coverage —the retail segment of marketing is looked at through the wrong end of the telescope. Marketing men and authors of marketing and advertising textbooks talk earnestly of the consumer-oriented view of business; but, down on the firing line, where the retailer faces the consumer, the retail merchant receives little help from the marketing men. They are busy telling the manufacturer how to sell the consumer and how to win the trade battle, but there is little real direction for the retailer from the experts. Reference to the retailer is usually included in a discussion of the "marketing mix" for the national advertiser, advising him on how to furnish some aids to his distributors.

It would seem then that there is real void to fill, by bringing some of marketing's thoughtful analysis to the field of retailing. Recent events have shown that the economy is not always on the rise, and a scatter-approach to retail advertising will not suffice. It is necessary to lay out the options in retail advertising and attendant promotions for retail-store management, large or small. It is necessary to give them an opportunity to see the long-view possibilities as well as what can be done day to day. Retail merchants are, after all, the last link in the marketing chain as it reaches out to the consumer. *Retailers are the sellers.*

It is hoped that this book can provide a current approach to this important subject. It must provide this approach in a way that will be deep enough to interest professional retail management, yet clear and simple enough to serve as a text for students who seek to enter the field—whether as "juniors" in retail management or directly in the area of retail advertising.

ii

Nothing in the foregoing is meant to suggest that there are no books devoted to retail advertising and promotion. There are indeed. But they are few in number compared to those that cover the *national* field. Moreover, the ones that do exist are either not current or not clear and easy to read.

To anyone who has worked with or taught classes of young students, it must be apparent that, while they will accept basic principles, these principles must be set in the framework of *today.* In their own idiom, the rules must be "NOW!" Then they will try them, test them, and finally accept them. One cannot simply present guidelines and show ten-year-old examples, however apt; nor can one say, "They have always worked." The students want to see these principles at work in their own world, now.

With a subject as exciting as retail advertising, why should the readers of such a text go to sleep over the reading? Why should the student get lost in heavy-handed meanderings? It is a challenge to keep the subject current, clear, and alive. It is essential if the student is expected to complete the readings.

iii

This leads naturally into a discussion of how this book was undertaken. There seemed to be only one way to be sure that principles would be real and material would be current—that one way was to go out and ask questions.

Through the kind and intelligent offices of the nationwide news bureaus of Fairchild Publications, a questionnaire, prepared by the author, was presented to leading retailers across the country. The retailers were chosen so as to be representative of the whole country, to be of various sizes, from "single ownership" to corporate, multi-branched stores, and covered several types of retailing: specialty stores, department stores, chain, discount, and variety stores. In addition, special study was devoted to stores in the huge shopping centers.

The questions covered the following general subjects: organization of the advertising department; methods of planning and budgeting; possible use of television and (if used) how handled; brand-store advertising; cooperative advertising. Two final questions were asked, one about the projected needs of the last years of our century, and another about the greatest service retail promotion could render in the same period.

Since the questionnaire was confidential, the results will be used throughout the book without reference to any retailer-source. Nevertheless, credit must go to the many fine stores whose executives took the time to supply valuable information.

Thus, in the area of advertising and promotion departments, in the titles and duties of personnel, in the use of media (and especially television), the recommendations made here incorporate some of the reports of what is being done across the country. As could be expected, the reports differed mostly accordingly to the size and type of the retail operation, not according to geographical location. This, too, will be reflected in the text.

As noted above a final set of questions asked the retail executive to comment, if he wished, on what would be the greatest service retail advertising could perform in the last decades of the century —for the consumer and for the retailer; and what the respondent believed would be retail advertising's greatest need.

Almost without exception, those who replied stated that the greatest service they could perform through their advertising was to educate and inform the consumer.

As to their greatest need, once again the answers clustered around *people*, the need for concerned, informed, and trained personnel.

Thus in searching for answers to general questions, the reinforcement and specific justification for this book were disclosed by the research—the quest for young people, educated and eager to handle advertising and promotion at the retail level.

iv

Of the many ways the material of this book could be presented, there were two that were considered.

First, when a young employee comes into the Advertising Department, if he* is not given tear-sheets to file, he is lucky. Certainly, the first writing jobs are limited; perhaps they include copy for a basement product, a small advertisement for an accessory department, or a 300-line advertisement for a budget dress.

And so, a book could start out by talking about how to write an advertisement for the basement, for a handbag, or the like. But frankly, the author could not comfortably write such a book. In the firm belief that writing copy for a $15 handbag takes as much skill as writing copy for a $150 coat, we have almost no choice but to abandon the method that is parallel to the job opportunity.

The method selected is to take the large view first; *i.e.*, to talk about advertising and where it fits into today's economy, with the

---

* Let the author, a woman, apologize at the outset and once and for all for adopting the traditional English custom of using the *masculine* pronoun as having a universal sense. We recognize the injustice to the female gender, but could not accept the cumbersome "he/she," "him/her." At times in talking of the consumer, "she" is used, for the shopper is frequently a woman.

service to the consumer and its function in retailing in all its various forms and developments.

Special emphasis is given to advertising as a communication from the store, as "communicator," to the consumer, as "communicant," through the chosen medium and by means of a stated message. Included as a separate chapter is a discussion of consumer buying habits, related to the growing trend of "consumerism" and to principles of selling as they best serve the consumer.

It should be noted that an awareness of the consumer has become almost an obsessive subject for a successful merchant today. Accordingly, it is a recurring theme in many other chapters of this book.

Then, consideration is given to the place that advertising holds in the retail-store structure, with its departmental organization and the responsibilities of its personnel. Closely bound to this subject will be a brief discussion of career opportunities. Planning for long-range objectives and immediate goals claim attention, too.

In the section on budget and media, several chapters cover the general decision-making responsibilities, methods of arriving at an advertising appropriation, and a discussion of store activities in general promotion and in cooperative advertising. Media planning and the considerations that lead to decisions on specific schedules are covered. One chapter here positions the store itself (and its branches) as a medium, and covers the coordination of in-store promotions and activities. (This subject, in fact, finds a place in more than one chapter and section.)

In the section devoted to the creation of advertising, attention is given to getting ideas, to formulating themes, to determining appeals, and to conveying the selling message in copy and artwork.

Innovative in *retail* marketing, although not necessarily new in the field of marketing in general, is a discussion of advertising's *total message as the configuration*, which becomes a concept particularly important in the chapter on visual elements.

A section on production covers print and broadcasting with a a totally retail slant, eliminating the endless discussions of costly production, whether of print or television, that is always entailed in national advertising.

As mentioned before, the coordination of all promotional activities is again referred to as a strong consideration in the creative aspects of advertising.

A section on testing and measuring results begins to bring the book to a close. A quick look at some legal and ethical restrictions and a discussion of the role of the retail store as a community-force for good finally bring the reader to the concluding paragraphs.

It is hoped that this brief preview will appear as logical and reasonable to the reader as it does to the author.

v

Some discussion may be appropriate as how best to use this book.

For the instructor who employs this book as a text, it is hoped that it will provide principles for which he and his students can find even more current examples than are included in the illustrative material. This kind of relevance is highly important to lend credence and a sense of immediacy to the pages.

If it is to be read by a practitioner in advertising, it can be read straight through, cover to cover. In this case, the reader's own background will supply more than enough examples to enliven the principles. He may agree; he may mentally argue; but it is hoped he will be stimulated.

PART ONE

ADVERTISING
IN TODAY'S
RETAIL WORLD

The retail world of today requires trained decisions in advertising. In an opening to this wide subject, the chapters in this section will define the terms to be used, in both retailing and advertising. Another chapter will cover the special functions of retail advertising and the services it performs for the store. A separate chapter will discuss the value and importance of advertising for the retail customer, the all-important consumer.

Finally, a chapter will review new developments in retailing, with their special advertising needs.

1

ADVERTISING AND RETAILING

How does the retailer look at "advertising?" How does he define the term? Who is this "retailer?" He certainly may be, if not defined, described.

Advertising is generally understood to be the communication through public media, in paid-for time and space, of a message from one source to another, with the specific purpose of persuading, convincing, and leading to some favorable action. Accepted definitions have always inserted the phrase "non-personal" as a limiting factor of the advertising communication.[1] This is not completely valid as a flat statement without qualification. One of the strongest advertising media is television, with its personal communication between a popular announcer or star and the public sitting more or less attentively in its living rooms. What is non-personal about that? In the sense, of course, that selling across the counter is truly *personal*, we may probably, for want of a better word, keep the old limitation "non-personal," but with new implications.

Thus, a satisfactory and up-to-date definition can be stated this way:

"Advertising is any paid-for form of communication in public media, by an identified sponsor, about ideas, goods, or services. Its purpose is to create favorable attitudes and acceptance, or to influence or induce sales. It is nonpersonal in the sense that it excludes face-to-face selling."

The generally accepted "public media" include space in newspapers and magazines, time over the radio or television stations, billboards, and transit facility posters. Also included are direct mail and handbills. This list seems to exclude only word-of-mouth communication, a form of promotion that falls either under advertising or publicity. Store signs are part of the display function.

Breaking with tradition, this text will include *the store itself as a medium* (although not a *public* medium). Later chapters will cover the store-wide promotion and advertising's place therein.

Additional elements of the definition still remain to be defined.

Modern studies in the psychology of the marketplace recognize "communication" as a multiple process which can be graphically illustrated (see Fig. 1).

The process starts with the sender and his decision to send a message. In a very literal sense, he deliberately wishes to "make waves." He starts the process, but from that point on, the process itself takes over.

The sender must have in mind, the more clearly the better, the recipient of his message. For the retail merchant, the recipient of

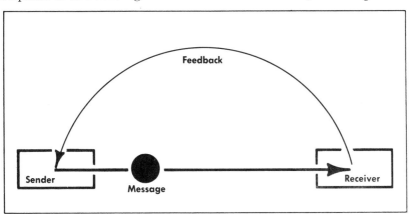

FIG. 1　THE PROCESS OF COMMUNICATION

his message may be the entire body of his present or his potential customers. These are "local" people, but only in a comparative sense. As opposed to the widespread market of national advertising, the retail advertiser can set reasonable geographical limits to his market. As shopping centers grow—and already more than 50 percent of all retail sales takes place in a shopping center,[2] the local nature of the retailer's customers will continually widen to take in the population that encircles the center. Distances will be measured in terms of time (to reach the center through varying degrees of traffic), rather than in terms of miles. The retailer in such a center must enlarge his horizons accordingly.

To continue with the Communication Chart (Fig. 1), the message and the medium are next to be considered. Despite Marshall McLuhan,[3] they can and must be separate for purposes of discussion, and yet the juxtaposition of the two in itself deserves mention.

The sender (the retailer) has a selling message to get to the recipient (the customer). His medium can be any of the channels already briefly catalogued. As he selects and uses one medium in preference to another (newspaper rather than radio, billboard rather than handbill, etc.), he will find that his message is somewhat altered by the very medium he selects. The immediacy of the daily newspaper, the slow, long pull of a magazine, the insistent intrusion of television: each has its effect on the message as it is received.

In addition to these elements, there is the reaction of the consumer after the message is received. Often called "feedback," the reaction or reply in general is evidence that the message has reached the target. If that reaction is positive, whether it be a pleased attitude, a favorable acceptance, the remembering of a brand name, a store name, a need, or finally an outright decision to buy—the sender can be satisfied that the communications cycle has been successfully completed.

It is in this sense of a total cycle that we wish to discuss retail advertising, to talk about how it works, and how the retailer can make it work better and more uniformly. If the reaction doesn't come within a reasonable time, the whole process would seem to have been wasted. A large proportion of retail advertising has as its goal immediate sales. For this kind of advertising communication, measurement is comparatively simple. But, for many other advertisements, goals may not be "immediate sales" at all. For these there are no easy answers. Attitudes and acceptance can be measured, and these can point to the level of success or failure. But special effort must be made to set up and complete the tests, and too few retailers take the time or spend the money to set up a testing program.

Another essential question to be answered is, "Who is the 'retailer'?" He is anyone who is individually engaged in running a store and selling a variety of goods to the American consumer. The "retailer" may, on the other hand, be a corporate body, yet still be engaged in the same task as the single store owner. The "retailer" may operate from a small shop with 100-foot frontage on a New York City street, or a village in Vermont or California or Indiana. He may run his business from a shopping mall near Albany or Seattle, or not far from Waikiki in Honolulu. The retail business may consist of one store or many. No matter—each one is occupied with turning a profit in a more or less hectic, frenetic business among an increasingly more intelligent, more aware, and more wary consumer-public. Each needs advertising and other forms of promotion to reach out his hand a greater distance, to increase the strength of his voice as he—no longer literally, but still realistically—calls out his wares.

It is in bringing these two together, advertising and the retailer, that the answers to the questionnaires disclosed some changes of pattern, depending mainly on the *size* of the business. It gave some answers to the question, "What does the retailer mean to include when he says 'advertising'?"

From medium-sized retail operations (about $50 million as a base), up to and throughout the ranks of the giants, the retailer gives the same definition and scope to the advertising function that was indicated many paragraphs back. In stores of this size, there are other departments staffed separately to handle publicity and display functions.

On the other hand, the smaller stores use the word "advertising" to include what is more properly defined as "sales promotion." They include in one department, under one functioning head, the tasks of advertising plus those of publicity and display. Some, un-schooled in professional terminology, are not aware that a distinction should be made.

It is always true that *all* stores from the boutique type to a mammoth department store have practically the same general functions to perform to make the store go round. The difference lies in the scope of the activity, and the consequent number of people employed to do the various jobs.

In the large department stores, *Advertising* is a separate department within the Sales Promotion Division. *Publicity* is quite separate, as is *Display* . . . and the Display Department may, in fact, actually be situated away from the main selling site.

In a small store, however, the advertising function is carried through by the owner (or his wife), who also handles any publicity and special events that may happen along. Should there be a possibility of participation in a local fashion show, generally the owner handles it, may break away to letter a sign for his store, and may also write a brief paragraph for the local newspaper. Thus, the whole Sales Promotion operation is handled by one person.

Perhaps, in order to mark the boundaries of *advertising*, we ought to say at once what it does *not* include: It does not cover *display*, whether window or interior. While it should not include copy for signs, frequently (in moderate-to-small stores) the advertising department *is* expected to include the "wording" for both window and interior cards.

It does not include the writing of *publicity* releases. The whole publicity function is by its very nature something quite different and apart from advertising. Except in the case of single ownership of a small store, this is one responsibility that is kept separate (and properly so) from *advertising*.

It does not include copy for *fashion shows*. Invariably, the fashion director or stylist writes her own commentary.

Finally, the *creation of special events* does not fall into the Advertising Department's area of responsibility. Certainly, however, most special events require advertising, and to this extent the department would be involved.

Thus advertising is clearly specialized, but unquestionably has a "synergistic" function of leadership and counseling in all the promotional activities.

FOOTNOTES

[1] Milton, Shirley F., *Advertising Copywriting*, Oceana Publications, Dobbs Ferry, N.Y., 1969.

[2] Information about shopping centers has come largely from International Council of Shopping Centers (ICSC).

[3] McLuhan, Marshall, *Understanding Media: The Extensions of Man*, McGraw-Hill Book Company, New York, 1964.

2

FUNCTIONS
OF A RETAIL ADVERTISING DEPARTMENT

We come logically to the question of what services advertising performs in the retail store. Effective retail advertising has an immediacy of purpose. It literally brings customers into the store and is responsible for immediate sales on advertised products. Advertising inserted in newspapers on Sunday is expected to bring action on Monday. What is advertised today is supposed to move out tomorrow.

But every store wants something more than that. A retail business wants to be "in the reckoning" on the day after tomorrow and next year and the years after that.

Accordingly, retail advertising is also charged with the specific job of selling the store as a good place, an interesting place at which to stop. Stores have personalities, as well as their special places in the community. (If they do not, they do not belong in business nor will they last long.)

One store may offer vast assortments; another low prices; another superior service; still another may take a stand as a leader in fashion. Some few great stores, in addition to sound merchandising and services, have built a place for themselves as an integral part of their community. Customers choose to shop in these stores *be-*

cause they recognize the store's understanding of neighborhood, village, or city concerns.

Whatever special place the store chooses to occupy, it depends upon its advertising to advance its personality or image. Thus, retail advertising builds store name as surely as national advertising builds brand name.

The institutional advertising of a store does this as its complete function. But the product advertising of a store, too, should sell the store to some extent in every merchandise advertisement.

This is an important function for advertising, especially with today's marketing practices. Years ago, manufacturers would offer "exclusives" to a store: *i.e.*, the exclusive right to handle a given brand. Today, "exclusives" are rare, and where they exist they usually refer to specific styles within a brand, not to the total brand line. And so it is important for a store not only to say, "Come in and see this new Brand X fashion!" The store must also say, "See it here and buy it here!" Why *here?* . . . Because this is a most satisfactory store in which to shop.

The word "satisfactory" was used deliberately, because customers will find satisfaction in different facets of the retailing operation. Retail advertising should communicate whatever the store's management feels the store is all about.

Not only through the words of the message, but also through the artwork and typography, the store's advertising should convey its fashion leadership, or low prices, or great variety, or quality. For the stores that have come to be linked with their cities of origin, a reasonable portion of the institutional budget should be allocated for community relations advertising. (These concepts are simply touched upon here to make the idea of institutional advertising clear. They will be enlarged upon in the appropriate sections.)

In its product advertising, a retail store should tell the public what merchandise its buyers have gathered together to sell. It can urge customers to come at once, or suggest that they drop in soon for seasonal merchandise.

Of course, retail advertising can announce sales and special promotions, too. These are planned as traffic builders, and without advertising they may almost be said not to exist, or to exist in a deliberately limited way. It takes the advertising to get the word out.

Through direct mail advertising, the store can reach its special family of customers: the charge-account customer. It can enlarge its roster of potential customers, and it can actually make new customers. It can let them in on special promotions and sales. Sometimes charge customers are given first notice of a sale, or first opportunity to choose from sales merchandise.

This avenue of communication also permits the store to reach out geographically beyond its normal transportation routes. (It is unnecessary to do more than mention Sears and Montgomery Ward's in this connection.)

Clearances at end of season, or of overstocked merchandise, depend on advertising, too, to start the ball rolling in getting the customer into the store.

Clearly, in a catalog of the functions of advertising, no one can include every possible purpose. Perhaps this list does no more than scratch the surface. An attempt will be made, nevertheless, to sum up. Some clear-cut functions of advertising include:

1. Communicating the store personality
2. Indicating the store's place in the community
3. Building store name
4. Stressing the importance of shopping "here"
5. Telling the news about the merchandise
6. Announcing sales and promotions
7. Building traffic
8. Reaching charge customers
9. Reaching customers beyond the normal transit pattern
10. Winning new customers.

3

ADVERTISING
SERVES THE CONSUMER

Today "consumerism" is more than a government catchword. The concept that business must serve the consumer has been generally accepted as a phrase for a long time. Today, *it must be acted upon* and must become *a by-word* for the retailer, in order to conduct a successful business.

The consumer will be the subject of further study throughout the ensuing chapters. At this point, we want to discuss how retail advertising serves the consumer and what is the nature of the service it provides.

The average consumer looks through the local newspaper regularly to see what the stores have to offer.

For basic food needs, she checks supermarket advertising that may occur daily, but more often is to be found on the day before the neighborhood's big weekly food-shopping day. She checks the advertisements of the various stores and notes comparative prices. She may take notice of the meat, produce, or dairy specials. Given equally convenient locations, she will plan to shop where the "special" suits her family's food needs and likes, and where the price is right. If the "special" provides a lower price for a luxury or favorite food, she may decide to stock her freezer. At any rate, she can, if she wishes, be armed before she leaves the house with information on "best prices," "best buys," and so forth.

ILLUSTRATION I   Customer Intelligence

Thus, in the casual skimming of supermarket advertising, the housewife is taking advantage of advertising's services. She receives information about products, varieties, prices. She can build her menu for the week based upon the buys that the ads offer her. The customer (the consumer) can, in effect, perform armchair comparative shopping.

Sometimes, indeed frequently, local supermarkets distribute, via direct mail or hand delivery, their own flyers, advertising set up as a four- or eight-page news bulletin that gives the neighborhood customer similar information—not, of course, on a comparative basis.

Moving from the advertising of food necessities to that of apparel, furniture, appliances, and even cars, we are entering into fields where retail advertising provides other important services to the consumer, while still including the comparative-shopping possibilities already suggested.

In advertisements for appliances, the family finds out who carries the brand which they have heard and read about in national advertising (on radio or television, or in newspapers or magazines). The retail store says in effect, "We have Brand A refrigerator."

For "big-ticket" items (like appliances and furniture), the store's advertising usually brings news of selling price and terms of selling. It answers the current question, "Can we charge it"? And for such items the advertisements give basic information, for instance, on construction, special features, guarantees, and so on.

In furniture, we move into another area where the consumer needs help—and oddly enough, an area not so far from fashion-points in apparel. Here the consumer wants to know about periods, styles, what goes with what. If she will look at available advertising she will begin to see how the retail store presents its merchandise and she can gain useful information.

In apparel, fashion comes into its own, and here, while certain purchases are necessary, the choice rests upon taste. The retail store can offer actual education in taste, in what's new, what's "in," what goes with what, how to accessorize.

Again, from all the departments of a department store, and from all kinds of specialty stores, the consumer is bombarded with fashion and construction details, price promotions, "price facts," to compare from one store to another.

In all areas of merchandising, retail advertising brings news of new products, and suggests items for labor-saving, more efficient ways of doing daily tasks.

Even in the area of stable merchandise, store advertisements act as reminders to "fill in." In January and August "white sales" from New York City to Honolulu, advertisements remind the housewife to replace worn-out linens, to put a new sparkle in the bedroom or dining area. At the change of seasons, gas stations remind newspaper readers and radio and television listeners to get the services that winterize the car, or prepare it for long trips. Safety measures can be suggested in retail advertising. Advertising of summer needs from a lawnmower to suntan lotion can be welcome reminders for the consumer.

All price promotions and clearances in all fields of retailing are brought to the consumer by advertising. It is to the customer's advantage to look into these clearances that often occur at the end of the store-buyer's season, but at the height of the season of the consumer's need.

All of this presupposes an intelligent consumer who *will* read competing advertising with a critical eye and an analytical brain. See illustration 1, page 12.

To summarize, retail advertising performs a number of real services to the consumer by:

    1.   Permitting the consumer to check food prices on an outright, as well as a comparative, basis
    2.   Providing an opportunity for at-home selection of best buys and favorite brands
    3.   Advising where to buy nationally advertised items
    4.   Listing construction facts and special features
    5.   Informing as to prices and plans for "charging"
    6.   Supplying details on periods, good taste, and fashion preferences
    7.   Letting her know what is current in fashion, where to get it, and how much it will cost
    8.   Reminding her of needed stable merchandise

9.   Reminding the consumer of safety measures for cars, large home appliances, summer or winter needs

10.   Advising her of special low prices often at the height of the season.

If further evidence is needed to prove the services that advertising provides for the consumer, we cite the study conducted for the Bureau of Advertising, ANPA (American Newspaper Publishers Association, 1968). In a series of interviews developed in this study, 92% of those interviewed indicated that advertising read

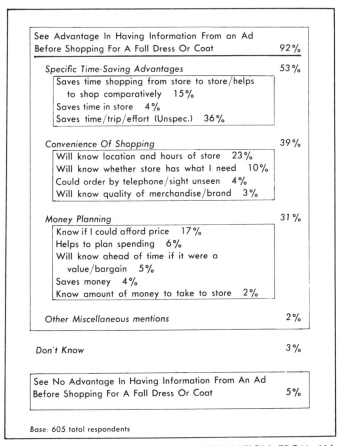

See Advantage In Having Information From an Ad Before Shopping For A Fall Dress Or Coat	92%
Specific Time-Saving Advantages	53%
Saves time shopping from store to store/helps to shop comparatively 15%	
Saves time in store 4%	
Saves time/trip/effort (Unspec.) 36%	
Convenience Of Shopping	39%
Will know location and hours of store 23%	
Will know whether store has what I need 10%	
Could order by telephone/sight unseen 4%	
Will know quality of merchandise/brand 3%	
Money Planning	31%
Know if I could afford price 17%	
Helps to plan spending 6%	
Will know ahead of time if it were a value/bargain 5%	
Saves money 4%	
Know amount of money to take to store 2%	
Other Miscellaneous mentions	2%
Don't Know	3%
See No Advantage In Having Information From An Ad Before Shopping For A Fall Dress Or Coat	5%

Base: 605 total respondents

FIG.   2   ADVANTAGES OF HAVING INFORMATION FROM AN AD BEFORE SHOPPING FOR A FALL DRESS OR COAT

before a shopping trip gave them needed and valuable information (Fig. 2).

The growth of consumer satisfaction in retail purchases and the consequent consumer confidence which leads to steady business growth can be expressed graphically (Fig. 3).

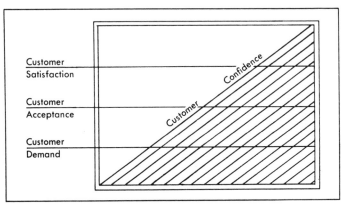

FIG. 3   A CHART TO SHOW MOUNTING CUSTOMER CONFIDENCE

4

CURRENT AND NEW DEVELOPMENTS

Retail advertising, like retailing itself, is most successful when it fulfills a real need for the consumer. New developments have come into view because the consumer seemed to evidence a need for some different way to shop. The retail advertising that follows current retail developments will change, too. There is a clear implication here that the kind of advertising needed will follow the kind of store operation that is set up.

Today we have certain clear trends—not new if "new" means two or three years—but certainly current and of "today." One trend is that towards the clustering of independent stores in what are variously called shopping centers, plazas, malls, and sometimes farmers' markets. More and more shopping is being done in these enclaves of retailing. Larger and larger sites are being built up for that use.

(Yet, even as this book goes to press, there are forecasts that stormy weather is ahead for "larger and larger" shopping centers. Environmentalists and ecology-minded communities are protesting the acquisition of the huge tracts that successful shopping centers need. Government regulations appear to be limiting the use of cars, and the fuel shortage is lessening the free availability of gasoline. Yet both cars and the gasoline they need are a life-line to these centers. The modern retailer must take a hard look at what lies ahead in the mid- and late-Seventies.)

Certainly not new, but having an interesting development now is the multi-division store, with the original store often in the heart of a downtown area wholly given over to business, and its branches scattered throughout nearby suburbs. And lately, we find a properly called *new trend:* that of branches of leading stores opening up halfway across the country for an inter-state enterprise. And, to match that at the other extreme, is the opening up of branches of one store in separate neighborhoods of the same city, perhaps only a mile or two apart.

Then there is the rented department or franchise that has been a fact of retailing for several generations, but is being looked at today in a new way.

Finally, there is a reappearance of a merchandising gambit that would probably be strange to young people, but not to their parents, *i.e.,* the bargain basement.

While the principles of advertising do not change, the handling of advertising for each type of operation will differ as would be expected, so that it can serve its special retailing function best.

The Shopping Center

To a great extent, the geographical location of a store in a shopping center does not change the essential identity of that store's advertising. The fact of location enters into the advertising done for a center or mall as a whole. In the more sophisticated centers, rather than in the farmers' market type, there is no frequent advertising in which all stores participate. This rule does not apply to the opening of such a center. At that time, for weeks, even months, prior to the "big day," there will be center-wide advertising, and lots of it.

At Christmas and Easter, and at other big selling seasons, there will always be some multi-store advertising.

Generally, a Promotion Office is set up at the headquarters of the center to handle public relations. The central promotion office will also plan and implement center-wide displays for special seasonal promotions and advertising that are cooperatively budgeted and funded. Frequently, the costs are allocated on a basis of square footage; sometimes, on projected sales volume, to be adjusted at regularly stated intervals. Additional funds are often supplied by the corporate management of the center as a whole.

Although not strictly "advertising," there is certainly center-wide promotion going on some place, constantly. In a sense this is a type of horizontal cooperative promotion and advertising with all stores participating in activities and costs (see Chapter 10).

The Multi-Branched Store

In the multi-branched operation, the most frequent handling of advertising is on a "total-store" basis; that is, a central advertising department is located (usually) in the old center-city store, to plan advertising for itself and all branches. The only concession to store-location differences in this method is a reference (as needed) to the presence or absence of certain merchandise in certain branchs.

Of course, as multi-branching reaches out in actual number of miles separating branch from home store, and as these branches begin to crop up in different cities, the advertising for each far-away branch must be autonomous for that store.

Certainly, the Chicago Bonwit Teller won't carry the same advertising as does the New York store. Sometimes, because of the suitability of some merchandise, it may happen to advertise the same fashion. This is still done autonomously and, to repeat, expresses the needs of the local store, rather than having any reference to the parent store.

Rented Departments and Franchises

Here we have a problem that can be solved either store by store or franchise by franchise. We are all familiar with the large food franchises, like Howard Johnson, whose decor, exteriors, and advertising are dictated by the central organization and are happily followed by the individual stores and restaurants.

In retail department stores, however, their own sense of identity is and should be so strong as to preclude a nationwide, across-the-board single identity for rented departments. In fact, whether by design or circumstances, the retail store rarely promotes the fact of the rented nature of the departments. Rather it advertises the department as an integral part of the store. The promotions and advertising for such departments are folded into the total store promotion-mix. The gain here is obvious, for, as has been noted earlier, a store should be an important part of its own community; and the community should, for its part (if the store does the job correctly), accept each department of a store as having the quality and service it expects of the whole.

The Bargain Basement

In the early decades of this century, through the depression and indeed until the upswing of our country's economy, every large department store had a bargain basement. The merchandise was very low priced and frequently looked it. The advertisements were as crowded as the basement; they used heavy black type and shabby little line drawings. The look of the advertising was different from that of the upstairs store, and no wonder: it was distinctly the "poor relation."

In the 50's and 60's with the sense of financial wellbeing that swept the country, stores looked with a sorry eye on that shabby, crowded store footage "down there." Large department stores took a variety of steps to eliminate the low-priced department. Some redecorated the area, put in new lighting, and called it the "Budget Shops." Other stores redecorated a little differently and put in a "wilder" type of lighting, added some heavy-beat music, and named the new baby "Boutique This or That."

Then the 70's came in with a sagging economic picture. High taxes ate into what had appeared to be adequate salaries. Middle incomes seemed not so rosy; lower income families were on the welfare rolls in greater and greater numbers. Yet both classes expected and demanded fashion in apparel and in furnishings, and a lot of convenience in appliances. Moreover, in all merchandise areas, department stores found they needed a new reply to discount stores' inroads into their sales.

Several department stores have found an answer in the return to the low-priced, realistically budget-stocked departments located in the basements, all over again.[1]

These basement stores demand a special kind of advertising. They should have a style and a character different from that of the upstairs store. But tastes have changed from the old days. There is a higher level of interest in color and design among all income groups. Consumers, it has been said earlier and will be said again, are better educated at all levels than their parents. They will look to the advertising to find out what the values really are. Advertising will have to spread the word about these new low-priced spots; it will have to bring the shopper into the basement store. If the departments have been well stocked and merchandised, the shoppers can become customers.

CATV

CATV, community antenna television, offers a new dimension in television broadcasting to retailers for store commercials. CATV, also called "cable television" is, briefly, the boosting of a TV station's sending signal up and over obstructions, by means of a community antenna placed at some point or on some building taller than anything else surrounding it. Patrons or subscribers pay for the signal to be brought to their sets by means of cable (telephone wires). The results include these benefits:

1. A greater geographical area is reached by the present broadcasting stations, meaning wider radius and enlarged listenership.

2. The subscribers receive a sharp, clear picture of the present, commercial broadcasts.

3. On the specific channels that have been awarded to the companies providing the cable service, there is, and will be more, special interest broadcasting. Programs now being beamed cover special sportscasts, talk shows, and films with so-called adult content. (In New York, these special channels are 6, 8, and 10.)

The significance to the retailer lies in the future opening up of these stations to commercial advertisers. Some channels are accepting commercials now. To whatever extent this becomes a reality, the retailer will have a wide radius of listenership. He will, additionally, know that his commercial is being received with good sound and picture reproductions.

FOOTNOTE

[1] "The Return of the Bargain Basement," *Retail Memo*, September 17, 1971. (Bureau of Advertising, ANPA)

PART TWO

THE STRUCTURE
OF ADVERTISING

This section will be devoted to the structure of advertising. The opening chapter of the section will discuss the organization of advertising departments, their relationship to the total sales promotion effort, to the store as a whole, and, where useful, to advertising agencies. The next chapter will be devoted to career opportunities. Then, in a logical opening of the full discussion of the working of an Advertising Department in a retail store, two chapters will cover the subject of planning.

5

ORGANIZATION
OF A RETAIL ADVERTISING DEPARTMENT

In an earlier chapter in which terms were defined, some attention was given to what advertising does *not* include. Now let us look at the positive picture and discuss the dimensions of an advertising department in a retail department or specialty store of medium-to-large size; *i.e.*, in stores with a volume of $50 million and up.

A Fully Staffed Advertising Department

The department is headed by an advertising manager supported by these functionaries at least: copywriter(s), art director (and artists), traffic and production manager, and possibly a copy-typist. These people may carry the entire load of a sector alone; or in large stores, there may be a sizable department with mini-departments acting for different divisions, as the Appliance Division, Fashion Division, etc. Sometimes they cover even smaller units where the volume of business and advertising is so great as to make the load heavy. This changes from store to store. It is important, however, to understand the details of each function, rather than to try to establish how many people perform them.

The *Advertising Manager* supervises the entire department. He plans total store-wide and departmental campaigns on a long-range basis, and at a top management level. He reports, in a full-scale retail operation, to the sales promotion director (see Fig.4ª). More frequently than not, he sits in with the sales promotion director at top management planning meetings.

In his supervision of the work of his department, he is responsible for the completion of a six-month budget for the store as a whole and for all the merchandising divisions. These are based on merchandising and promotional plans set by the general merchandising management and the sales promotion manager.

It is his responsibility to assess advertising opportunities as they arise. He initiates institutional advertising and advertising of "whole-store" events.

The selection and economical buying of media space and time, which will be covered in a later portion of this book, is his responsibility.

The preparation and release of effective advertising copy (copy *per se* and appropriate artwork) that underscores and furthers the desired reputation of the store also come under his control. In fact, it is he who develops an advertising style for layout, artwork, and copy that should, in itself and at its best, convey the sense of the store's merchandising and service policies to the consumer.

Administering his department and establishing a sound, workable rapport with merchandising personnel, particularly with the buyers, are other important elements in his job.

Certainly high in importance and basic to his effectiveness is the continuing effort that the advertising manager must exercise to understand the consumers who are present or potential customers of *his* store.

Finally, under his supervision the department should set up and maintain files and scrap books of past and current advertising to serve as a reference for its own and other interested store personnel.

The *Copy Department,* or the *Copywriter,* is responsible for the preparation of all the written portion of an advertisement from headline to the store hours and address line. It, or he, is responsible for the whole of the script, music, and sound effects of radio advertising, and for the script, music, sound effects, and action of television commercials.

More than is perhaps implied in the previous paragraph, the copywriter is responsible more often than not for the *total concept* of the advertisement—a concept that will be interpreted by his own copy and the artwork.

The copywriters are expected to know how best to present the selling message in terms both of product benefit and consumer interest. Thus, it is most frequently the copywriter who is held accountable for the sales success of a given advertisement.

Whether rightly or wrongly so, the accountability exists at least in the department buyer's thinking. This will be referred to again in the chapter on planning.

In very large retail stores, there may be so much advertising that the large staff of copywriters is set up in groups under group heads; these in turn, report to a copy chief, who reports to the advertising manager. As had been indicated earlier in this chapter, these groups would logically correspond to and handle the advertising work of divisions of the whole store.

Thus, the groups will form natural teams of *specialists* in various sections of merchandising. This will depend, of course, on the size of the store and the number of copywriters on staff.

Where a store is engaged in a steady advertising program of radio and television, the grouping may be according to media, with certain copywriters handling print (again perhaps broken into groups) and others handling radio and television.

The *Art Director* in a retail advertising department is responsible for the layout of each advertisement produced; for the selection and ordering of the appropriate photography or illustration to complete the needed visual; for the selection of appropriate typography; and for the preparation of mechanicals (paste-ups) for the newspaper or engraver.

In some cases, large retail stores may operate their own photography studios right in the store, with photographers on salary. In this case, the photographers would very likely report to the sales promotion director for their overall functions, and to the art director for advertising. They may also work for other departments, certainly as a service arm of the Publicity Department. They would be involved in any fashion shows given by the store (both for publicity pictures and for record-keeping), and would be called upon as needed for "photography-of-record" of any store happening whether corporate or departmental.

As is true of all sections of the department, an important duty of the art director is to review and approve all proofs of advertising that come back to the department, making corrections and giving additional directions where necessary.

The *Traffic* and *Production* function (whether vested in two groups of people or in a single person) is responsible for the following:

Production, working closely with the Art Department, is responsible for the mechanical production of the advertisement. In print media (for retailers this means newspapers mainly) this entails having the artwork properly prepared for reproduction, the copy properly marked for typography, and the "mechanical" prepared. In the bulk of retail advertising which falls into newspapers, the production manager of a store works closely with his opposite number at the newspaper's plant. Where special advertising is especially prepared for a newspaper and always when the preparation is for a magazine, the production manager works with a typographer and an engraver.

It must be made clear that the Art Department (and usually an art director) prepares the material, and stipulates the type-style wanted, while the production manager carries out these instructions, working with the outside houses to an even greater extent than the art director.

Traffic insures the smooth flow of work to meet media deadlines. This means setting up and maintaining the necessary procedure through schedules to get merchandise from the "floor" to the Advertising Department on time, to schedule layouts, copy, artwork, typography, engravings (if involved), and approvals so that all media commitments are met on time. Traffic handles work orders and release orders for newspapers, and releases for magazine advertising.

Finally, most advertising departments have some clerical help, frequently a copy-typist and perhaps a filing clerk. If so, then it is the clerk's job to maintain the tremendous scrapbooks that many retail stores still keep.

An interesting piece of research could be instituted on the use of microfilm by retail stores to act as a memory bank for their advertising. This would take the place of scrapbooks and filing cabinets for all but the advertising of the immediate past.

Relation to Sales Promotion

Advertising, if not the right arm of sales promotion, certainly is its voicebox. It is the largest of the three departments that normally constitute a Sales Promotion Division (see Figs. 4ª, 4ᵇ). Its manager or director is and should be a close advisor of the Sales Promotion Division.

The Advertising Department is the "voicebox" of sales promotion because it speaks for the store, addressing its customers in paid-for space or time, through the medium that brings the store into the home, whether it be by daily newspaper or radio or television. It speaks out the message of the store, telling what products are offered, at what price, in what quantity. It tells of the services the store offers, and it invites the customer in to see the store and its products.

But not only is advertising the largest department in the Sales Promotion Division, it generally accounts for the largest single non-merchandising business expense.

The Display Department, with its responsibility for windows, interior display, and signs, after having initial expenditures, should run along at an even level of expense.

Publicity, with its important responsibility for maintaining good press relations, has the smallest expense of all. Publicity expense is basically limited to salaries and money outgo concomitant with its core-job, such as photography, printing, mailing, "expense account."

Special Events, so integral a part of getting good publicity for a store, for building traffic in the store, for generating goodwill among the customers, will have its own budget, planned event by event. In many large stores, Special Events has its own department manager and personnel. In smaller stores, it is part of the Publicity Department.

Fashion shows, falling partly into sales promotion and partly into merchandising, will have a specific budget charged against the department for which they are being planned.

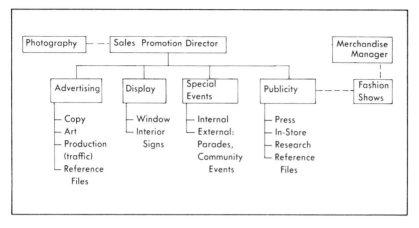

FIG. 4A   LARGE-STORE ORGANIZATION OF
A SALES PROMOTION DEPARTMENT

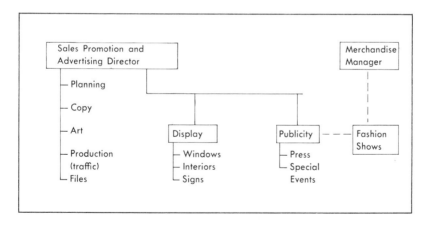

FIG. 4B   MEDIUM-SIZED STORE ORGANIZATION
OF A SALES PROMOTION DEPARTMENT

In the organization of the whole store, the Advertising Department works under the Sales Promotion Division, albeit independently within its own functions, to accomplish its goals. It prepares the monthly advertising plan, copies of which go to the merchandising managers and buyers. This working plan acts as a review and a reminder of what has already been set forth in the six-month plan. (Medium-sized and small stores may not work farther ahead than two or three months.)

As a reminder, it tells the buyer what the department previously agreed to advertise day by day within the given period. It tells him the size of advertisement for which he is scheduled, the medium or media in which it will appear, and roughly the cost of space (or time). (Additional details will be discussed in the chapters on planning.)

Any changes in the plan that can be accomplished without disturbing the overall pattern of the advertising program can be handled directly by buyer and advertising manager at this time. In large stores where many copywriters work under a group head, the communication between group head and buyer can be very close. In all stores, there should be frequent and cordial communication between the advertising manager and the merchandise managers.

In smaller stores, there may, in fact, be no sales promotion director as such. His duties of supervision, however, are assumed by the advertising director with advertising copywriters sometimes called upon to handle publicity, sign-writing, and fashion-show commentary. One cannot quarrel with the demands of "smallness" any more than with those of "bigness." Each imposes its own imperatives. The small stores' combining of several compartmentalized writing jobs into one is a way of functioning that must be recognized.

The value to the store lies in "getting the job done." The value to the copywriter lies in a widening of his skills. It is important, however, that the copywriter and advertising manager, too, recognize the differences. The copywriter is wearing several hats, and he would do well to move from one desk to another for the different jobs; or, if that is not possible, to keep very clearly in mind the vast differences in writing styles called for by each of these: advertising copy, publicity writing, fashion-show commentaries, and sign-writing.

Relationships with Agencies

It is appropriate here to discuss the place or the "non-place" the advertising agency holds in relation to retail advertising.

The advertising agency is an outside business—a group of professional people whose services are offered on a commission or commission-and-fee basis.

The services offered at no extra charge include planning, copywriting, art direction, advice on media selection, the economical purchasing of media, and suggestions for, and supervision of, research as needed. Services which are paid for include actual artwork, photography, illustrations, production costs, and field research. Time and space (actual costs of media) are, of course, billed to the client.

In some cases, especially in national advertising where media "buys" can run into millions, there is no extra expense involved in using an advertising agency. There are innumerable advantages, just a few of which include: skilled professional advice; the results of long and valuable experience; objectivity; ability to buy media for the clients with special know-how; and resultant savings.

National advertisers and their agencies plan advertising programs at least a year ahead and in most cases begin to produce actual advertisements four to six months before publication or airing. National advertisers, almost to a man, use agencies.

The retail advertiser, on the other hand, has uppermost in mind the rapid movement of his business. Retailers, moreover, put most of their advertising money into local newspapers. It is important, then, to have an Advertising Department right on tap, so that merchandise or price changes can be transmitted, sometimes right up to press time. There ought to be, as discussed a few paragraphs back, almost daily communication between buyers and advertising personnel. The buyer must, in addition, approve the advertisement at various stages.

All of this becomes an obstacle course when dealing with an agency.

In fact, for day-to-day product advertising, the fastest, most efficient way to handle the advertising is through an in-store department (such as has already been described).

There are retail stores which do use agencies and in many different ways.

First, medium-to-large retail stores may wish to work with an agency to plan and execute institutional advertising. This, of course, has none of the "this minute" frenzy of daily product advertising. It can and should be planned well in advance. Its approval does not depend on the harried buyer, but upon the advertising director, the sales promotion manager, and top management, who have (or must make) the time to discuss possibilities and alternatives, and choose the institutional campaign that best suits the store's long-range objectives.

Second, a store may use an agency to assist in a large special event, such as a "100th Anniversary." Again, planning is long term. In this situation, the early institutional advertising for such an event would be agency planned, while the simultaneous and follow-up product advertising should be handled by the store's own department in line with a general plan previously agreed upon.

Third, some stores use the partial services of a specialized agency, perhaps for the art direction, or for special production (beyond the capabilities of the local newspaper):

Fourth—and this should be carefully noted—as stores moved into the broadcast media, radio and television, they felt the need for specially qualified professional help in creating effective commercials. This was particularly true of television.

Retail advertising departments used to be entirely print-oriented. They understood newspapers particularly well. When their stores sought to expand into radio, and later into television, many copywriters and advertising managers, too, felt like fish out of water. They were willing to let the professionals take over.

For awhile, there seemed to be a trend towards more and more use of agencies. There is no accurate way to check, but some agencies have recently indicated disappointment with the potential of the retail field. They have stated that as advertising managers feel more at home with television, they are more anxious to take over the handling of commercials, and incorporate that function into the store's own department.

There are several reasons for this move. Advertising executives, in retail or elsewhere, are first and foremost interested in advertising, and anything that concerns advertising calls for their involvement in it. Next, there is the out-and-out familiarity already referred to. Led into the television studio by agency personnel, the retail adverising personnel—intelligent, interested, and alert—learn fast. And as time has moved on, retail copywriters have started coming into the field who are themselves of the broadcast generation. They have lived with radio and television all their thinking lives, and they are ready, as their predecessors were not, to take on broadcast assignments in their daily professional lives. These are all healthy signs. No one ought to be afraid of any part of his own chosen field. The retail stores can gain the same benefit from in-store broadcast experts, as they have, for so long, from in-store print experts.

As the Advertising Manager begins to feel at home in the medium of broadcast (whether or not he is over 30, and most are), he feels at home in the supervision of copywriters, of their output, and of the creativity called for by the storyboard. This, too, perhaps, must depend on the investment in and continuity of program his store will commit to broadcast plans.

Production of television commercials does not add measurably to the problem of agency or in-store handling, since commercials are produced by independent studios, usually selected by bid. Increased familiarity with the broadcast function would entail an advertising manager's increased ability to let out for bid, to exercise limited supervision, and to approve the actual production of the commercials.

6

CAREER OPPORTUNITIES

For the person interested in a career in retail advertising, there are certain goals to be set and some options as to the road to take.

First, the goals can be translated into job titles which lie in the Copy, Art, or Production Departments. Management and supervision must, of course, come later, with experience. For the sake of clear discussion, let us set a title for each one in the beginning stages of a career.

Goal	*Probable Starting Job*
Copywriter	Junior Copywriter; Typist
Art Director	Art Secretary
Production Manager	Production Assistant; File Clerk

The career track into copywriting is based upon writing skills and a good business sense. One without the other can give either a novelist on one hand, or a merchant on the other, but only the two together will yield a copywriter. The copywriter, as has been said, is generally expected to create the total concept of the advertisement, to understand the selling points of the product, and to know what motivates the consumer to buy. Accordingly, the junior copywriter ought to have, as a natural aptitude, a wide curiosity, a willingness to dig for facts, a feeling for people, a toughness that lets him accept criticism and come back fast with something better. He should be able to "target in" on a single product benefit and write about that facet of the merchandise before him.

He should have a reasonably good education. A college education is expected of him. Many junior college students have become interested in the field of retail advertising, and have been successful in landing and keeping desirable junior copywriting jobs, and moving on to jobs as full-fledged copywriters and into management.

The education should cover as much as possible of literature, to stimulate the imagination and provide a background. It should include psychology, sociology, marketing, and anything else that creates an alert, interested, inquiring mind.

It is sometimes hard to get a copywriting job as a first job; however, selling is fine training for it. In selling, one gets the contact with the consumer, feels the need to communicate salient characteristics and benefits of the product. Selling helps one *listen,* too, to discover what it really is that the consumer wants.

Jobs that lead to copywriting encompass almost anything you can get in an Advertising Department: typist, secretary, file clerk, receptionist (a job not usual in retail advertising, however).

For the career goal of Art Director, there is perhaps a more direct route: that through creative talent in illustration or photography. Even here, an art secretary's job can be helpful in getting to that first step. Art schools, junior colleges, four-year colleges all help prepare a talented young man or woman for a career in the unfortunately named field: Commercial Art. Here, the start can be (as has been noted) Art Secretary, or Junior Artist, then Art Assistant. Large departments have members of the art staff who do mechanicals (the precision paste-ups based upon the comprehensive layout that represents the last step before the newspaper or engraving shop takes over).

Young people who are interested in this field are always surprised to learn that "finishes," the actual illustrations or photographs, are never completed by the Art Director. Illustrators and photographers, frequently working free-lance or through an art studio, handle the completion of the planned artwork, for the approval of the Art Director.

For a job in Production, the road seems to be through on-the-job training. Certainly, any courses that are available in printing, typography, mechanical preparation of artwork can be helpful. The job calls for a perfectionist, someone willing to put in long hours and painstaking care to see that the department's advertising turns out as perfect in detail as it existed in the minds of the department members when it was planned. Last-minute corrections, early-morning proofs, buyer approvals . . . these are some of the by-products, as it were, of a production man's daily routine.

The job calls for integrity and loyalty to the store's best interests, for the production man can be bombarded by persuasive offers on the part of engravers, typographers, signmakers, and a host of other suppliers. It is the production manager who puts out bids, and in the case of booklets, brochures, store signs (sometimes), these can carry considerable weight. The Production Manager and his assistants must be of single purpose, and granite-faced to all suggestions that do not contribute to getting out a better job at an economical (not cheap) price. "You gotta love it!" . . . but if you do, it can be a highly rewarding job, without much outside credit given, except by members of the Advertising Department, who generally are grateful for a fine production manager.

(Broadcast production, as has been noted, is generally handled outside the retail advertising department.)

To sum up, most of the jobs in advertising call for on-the-job training. Careers in copy and art demand creative thinking, imagination applied to pragmatic merchandising, with all the study of people that you can get—through college courses and through constant and intelligent observation.

7

THE FRAMEWORK OF PLANNING

From the management point of view, the planning of retail advertising is possibly the most important aspect of the advertising
function (until the advertising appears, at any rate).

Every store will have *long-range* and *short-range* (or immediate)
plans. This author would like to propose the phrase *"middle-range
planning,"* adding it to the other two, and explaining it very shortly.
Each of these phrases needs explanation in the context of this
book, so that the ensuing discussions on each may start from the
point of understanding the semantics involved.

Long-range planning generally means one-year to five-year projections. A store, especially a large store with an inner-city location
and several branches, is certainly wise to look forward for a reasonable block of years and plan its growth. The sales-promotion director and advertising manager should be included in the early con-
ferences and should be expected to propose long-range promotional
plans. It is through appropriate promotion that a store can expect
to explain its future plans and its place in the community to the
very people who will interact with it for each other's gains; *i.e.,*
the consumer public.

Long-range plans today must not only include merchandising

and service policies (more of that later), but communal ambitions as well—how the store hopes to grow, where it plans its growth, the sources from which it expects to draw strength. The community today will tolerate only a *good* neighbor.

(In New York City, a store that planned a new edifice was led, by public opinion strongly vocalized, to participate in a subway-station improvement program. In the same period, another large store gave up its option on space in an area because neighborhood demands were too extreme to make building profitable.)

So community welfare must be built into the long-range plans. It is certainly useless to keep this a secret, so the promotion departments must shoulder their part of these plans, must advise the public, sometimes through publicity, but more directly and surely through advertising.

A store, too, must look ahead to the impact that external changes will have on its operation. Where is the population moving to in a given city? Is the center city becoming a slum, or is it being improved, modernized, given new life?

How is the population changing? Are there racial changes? Are there income changes? Age changes? Is this now a neighborhood of young career people, or is the trend running that way? Do they, as may be expected, live in studio apartments? Are there large apartments or single-dwelling "family" houses in the area? Is the area part of the business or financial district of the city? If we are discussing suburbs, is there room for parking, for later expansion?

These are some of the questions that a large, forward-looking store asks, and that it expects will be answered, not only for now and next year, but for perhaps five years hence. The answers must be present as a preliminary to laying its plans. If the answers are not available through labor statistics or from a city department, then research must be initiated and followed through.

These are the very questions that the Advertising Department must ask and have answered, too, for its plans must be made to capture the approval and, insofar as is possible, the loyalty of its body of prospective customers, as that multiple creature changes through the successive years.

Earlier we mentioned three areas of growth: a) as a member of the community b) in merchandising c) in services. Of course, all of these contribute to the profit-factor which the comptroller's department, in its turn, will have put on graphs for a look-ahead period.

In merchandising and services, the store's management and its merchandising team will use the research information to plan well into the coming years.

It may, to many stores, seem impossible to plan five years ahead. Certainly, exact merchandising, exact promotions, definite advertising plans are not what is meant here. Rather it is for management to look into the future at large economic and demographic developments that can perhaps be foretold for its own area, and to put this information to use.

Advertising, too, in addition to what has already been said, can look into the future and perhaps see where its "look" can be updated; where its logotype, layout, typography may be brought into line with the trend of visual art. With this kind of forward-sight, advertising can plan a slow series of changes that will not jar its own, present large body of loyal customers, but can begin to attract new younger groups, as well.

A large and (yes, really!) beloved store in New York City had until recently held on to a 35-year-old format that served it well for many years, but left an impression of the dowdy today. This store has been well advised to begin a change, holding fast its loyal admirers and beginning to win some of the young customers it deserves to have and to which its merchandise and service policies entitle it.

(In Chicago, a few years ago, a large store undertook long-term research into the future of its city and its part in the city life, taking demographic projections up to 1980. It then set up long-range promotional plans that were expected to take five years to mature. The changes in advertising alone included a change of type face, new media plans, and a new spirit in the copywriting.)

What definition can be given to "middle-range" planning? That is a term this author would like to give to the multi-month planning (less than a year) devoted to actual merchandise choice, media selection, budget considerations, and advertising schedules. This, in a few stores, is done by the year. In most stores, however, it is a *six-month plan*.

After the initial steps, it works on what may be called the zigzag method. (See Fig. 5.)

First, management, merchandise managers, sales promotion director, advertising manager all sit down to plan the store's six-month appropriation for promotion. This is often called the "whole-store plan." It looks at the store as a whole, plans store-wide promotions, includes institutional advertising, and assigns the total sales promotion appropriation. (Methods of arriving at a budget will follow in a later chapter.)

The sales promotion director and advertising manager next devote their attention to setting up a middle-range or six-month plan. Media contracts and budgets enter here, but must be discussed later.

The advertising manager, with his part of the promotional plan in front of him, must help set up divisional plans. Generally, he (or someone of his staff) prepares a chart showing each division and each buyer within that division what advertising has been done week by week within the parallel period of the previous years, and an estimate of what may be wanted for the coming year. Media plans and cost of space are shown.

FIG. 5   FLOW-CHART FOR MIDDLE-RANGE ADVERTISING PLANS
"THE ZIG-ZAG METHOD"

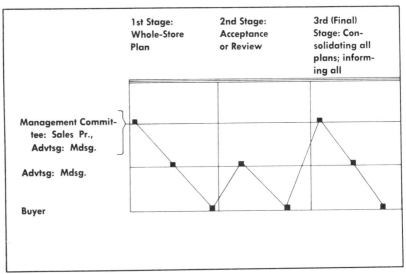

These are sent in several copies to the divisional merchandise managers, and through him to the merchandise managers and buyers (or direct to the buyers in some stores).

The buyers review the plans and, based upon the goals and information they have on their own and any directives from their divisional merchandise managers, they accept the Advertising Department's recommendations, or indicate what revisions they would like to see made. These preliminary plans then go back to the Advertising Department.

Here the plans are reviewed, tied together to be fitted into the plans for the whole store, into any image-building campaigns, and into the plan for media use already decided upon.

At a later date, the *short-range* plan goes into effect. The term is used to describe the immediate current planning of advertising anywhere from two to four weeks ahead, based upon the strong middle-range plans that have been developed and approved.

Within the short-range plan, the Advertising Department works on a monthly advertising chart, with reminders sent to the buyers (as noted above) re-stating the advertising that is planned for their departments. Finally, the buyer sends the merchandise and merchandise information to the Advertising Department for action.

8

PLANNING ADVERTISING STRATEGY

What constitutes a plan? Certain specific aspects apply to all plans whether they be business or pleasure, a trip to Europe or an advertising campaign. Informally stated, then, in order to plan, we must know:

    a) what we want
    b) where we want to go
    c) how we want to get there
    d) how much time we have
    e) how much money we can spend.

It is immediately apparent that several of these are inter-related. Money available may affect the time we take, and vice versa. The route taken will have something to do with both time and money, and so forth.

So, in preparing an advertising plan for the whole store (what is generally called advertising strategy), money and time are always inter-reacting with each other and affecting other concepts. And yet, we must take some one step first, and then another. We must plan, and we must put our plans, in business, into written form.

There are some very large differences between business and pleasure planning, of course. Among them is the fact that one may have a good time on an unplanned tour of Europe, but equivalent wanderings in a business venture would be financial suicide.

Russell Colley, in writing about advertising plans, puts the need this way:

> "In recent years, a number of companies have recognized the importance of marketing and advertising planning. Some have done an extremely thorough job of gathering and cataloging in great detail product and marketing information. Some of this information consists of available statistical and product data—'inside-out' information. Other segments of this information deal with the habits, characteristics, attitudes and motivations of *people* who comprise the market.
>
> "All of this information can be extremely valuable. But it is a misnomer to label such data a 'plan.' This is merely background information. The 'plan' itself may be only ten pages rather then ten pounds. And the essence of a plan is a goal. It represents, in a single page or paragraph, the *decision* which has grown out of months or even years of research, thinking and planning. It states in a few words.
>
> 'This is the message we want to deliver.
> 'This is the audience we want to reach.
> 'This is the accomplishment we expect to achieve'." [1]

Perhaps this is over-simplification, but it states clearly what is important. For retail advertising, which must conduct itself in a businesslike fashion and must work within given fiscal limits, we would set up the elements of a plan in a little different way, one which adds to Colley's goals to assemble clearer, more workable points for a retail-store advertising plan.

There are seven large areas that must be given consideration. After a listing here, each will be discussed at some length.

1.   The *goals and objectives* (short-term and long-term) of the store's advertising campaign.

2.   The *message content* that the advertising must convey.

3.   The *consumer* upon whom the store can appropriately look as a current or prospective customer.

4. The *media*, channels of communication, to be used in conveying that message (#2 above) to those consumers (#3 above).

5. The *budget* that will be needed for this campaign.

6. The *time* allotted for the campaign, both the length allowed and the season of year involved.

7. The *personnel* who will handle the advertising, within the store's department, or outside if an agency is used, wholly or in part.

8. *Evaluation.*

Goals and Objectives

Retail stores must have two main objectives in their advertising if they are to remain in business and keep that business profitable.

First, they must promote the sale of their merchandise. Second, they must build their store as a "total institution," fostering favorable attitudes towards their name and store to create the image of a friendly atmosphere and a good neighbor in the community.

Kenneth Collins,[2] one of the all-time greats in retail advertising, has said that *every* retail advertisement, however much it "sells" the product, must to some extent also sell the store. If not, your advertising is not building for future purchases.

In retail advertising, more clearly than in national or trade advertising, increased sales or immediate sales can be one of the valid gauges of effective advertising. But it must be borne in mind that advertising is not *ever wholly* responsible. Responsibility for increasing (or, perish the thought, decreasing) sales must rest on a total marketing spectrum: the general economy of the nation, the local economy of the area, competitors' activity, perhaps the financial market *that day*, strikes, the product itself, degree of acceptance of its national brand name, the store's housekeeping, the personnel, the location of the store, the transportation situation, the weather *that day*, and so forth. (Ask any retailer—his list of upsetting or augmenting factors is endless!)

Some specific objectives [3] include:

1. To announce a special reason for buying "now."

2.   To remind people to buy a given product, to suggest multiple-unit buying or larger sizes.

3.   To tie in, via advertising, with some special store event being promoted within the store and often in window displays, as well.

4.   To stimulate impulse sales.

5.   To create an awareness of the very existence of a product or brand, or of a new line, or of a new or up-dated department within the store.

6.   To create a favorable disposition toward the store.

7.   To implant information or attitudes regarding benefits and superior features of merchandise.

8.   To combat or offset competitive claims, to convert competition's customers to one's own store.

9.   To correct false impressions, misinformation and other obstacles to sales (to be used warily).

10.   To build familiarity and easy recognition of store's own brand and trademark.

11.   To build confidence in the store, which will pay off in years to come: to stress quality, dependability, service.

12.   To establish a "reputation platform" for launching new lines, new branches.

13.   To make steady customers out of occasional or sporadic customers.

14.   To encourage greater frequency of store visits.

15.   To offer mail orders, special payment terms.

With these goals in mind, we can move to the consideration of the next element in the advertising plan.

The Message Content

If every advertisement, in addition to anything else it does, must sell the store as an institution as well, then our message content must be based on a knowledge of the kind of store for which we are writing.

Stores may be classified by size, type, and leadership in a given area of merchandising.

To classify a store by size is more difficult than it would appear, simply because published figures usually include the volume of all members of a corporate group. "Inside" figures are disclosed, if at all, with much reluctance. Certainly, this book does not need to list stores to make a point. Volume above $50 million is "big." Volume between five million and 50 million is "medium"; between $500,000 and five million is "small"; and below the half-million, we normally find "family-owned" stores. Smaller yet are the "mom-and-pop" shops.

Classification by type is easier to arrive at. A "department store" is one whose merchandise includes both apparel and household goods. Marshall Field of Chicago is an example.

A "specialty store," however large, is one whose merchandise lies within the apparel group alone (as Bonwit Teller), or within the household furniture group (W. & J. Sloane, for example).

A "discount store" may fall into either category; many carry both "hard" and "soft" goods. (Korvette's in the New York area is an example.)

A "chain store" is one whose buying, merchandising, and promotional policies are directed from one central office, although the selling outlets may be located in one region of the country, or across the whole country. (Sears or J. C. Penney come to mind.)

A "family-owned" store is just what its name implies, owned by a close group, frequently related, with a store successfully run on modest lines—usually a single unit. If the store grows, the original store and its branches are most often found in one area or one region of the country.

A "mom-and-pop" shop is something very old and, in a way, something very new. This refers to a small, single-outlet store run by one or two people. In older days, it was indeed mother and father working together (or brothers and/or sisters). Today, as every college professor of merchandising knows, the young people are opening up their own versions of these shops and calling them boutiques. Today, it is most frequently two friends who pool their resources (money, brains, imagination—and some know-how) and open a shop.

Finally, we come to the classification of degree of leadership that the store holds in its chosen field. This makes a strong difference in the content of the advertising message the store must deliver.

In furniture, in automobiles, in fashion apparel, there are stores which are leaders in their area, others which are middle-of-the-road, and still others which follow.

The leaders present the *news* in fashions for men, for women, in children's wear, in furniture, in appliances, etc. Price is secondary. Service is usually stressed, as is a certain exclusivity. These are not the stores that present a message of large assortments. On the contrary, everything is one or a few of a kind.

Other stores take the middle of the road. They present merchandise that has been accepted and is of top quality. Their prices are moderate and their strength is in the formula: *quality plus price equals value.* Many stores in this group base their reputations on huge assortments.

The third group of stores is set up to follow, offering accepted merchandise, but pressing hard on a *low price factor.* Each has its place in the retail-store community and, as we shall see further on, each has its loyal customers.

A fourth category not included above rests on the promotion-mindedness of stores. For some years, this category provided for a valid distinction among stores. They were divided into promotional, non-promotional, and semi-promotional. In today's market and in this author's opinion, this is no longer realistic. All stores that open their doors to the public are promotion-minded. Both the institutional image and the merchandise being promoted can range from the great fashion leadership stores at one end of a scale to the discount stores at the other end. Each promotes in a different and distinctive way, but the point is *each promotes!*

The old picture of the upper-class store as a kind of Victorian lady (she never got her name in the paper except for engagement, wedding, and death) does not exist today. Nieman-Marcus, a fashion leader known as such throughout this country, promotes its name and its merchandise with *hoopla* unexcelled by any. What else are "his and her camels," a "Noah's Ark" built life-size, and the like? Saks-Fifth Avenue promotes exclusive designers; Ohrbach's promotes copies. Today, no store simply rests on its laurels.

Thus, size, type, and leadership status will affect the retail message. The image of itself that the store wishes to project will enter into the message content.

The merchandise the store has to offer is the heart of the product advertising.

Again, the merchandise the store presents in its advertising has already been selected on the basis of the kind of store it is. The message about the merchandise grows out of the "product" objectives, and many of these have been previously listed. The product and its selling points (to be defined in Chapter 14) are other important parts of the message content.

Finally, the theme—sales, savings, Christmas, and so on—helps to shape the message.

The Consumer: The Target Audience

Who are the consumers a given store can reasonably expect to reach and to affect in a positive way? This target audience ought to be the deep concern of the entire store from top management down. In large stores, this group of current and prospective customers is the subject of intensive research and study. In smaller stores, the formal research may be lacking, but the interest is still very much present.

Every business today spends a respectable proportion of its research budget on gathering information on the kind of consumer who will use its products.

Retailing, learning more and more how to "hedge its bets," has learned, too, how valuable consumer research can be for its own needs.

Large retail stores and medium-sized retail stores, too, often operating under the umbrella of a huge parent corporation, know that they must have a profile of their own consumers. For these stores a whole array of secondary sources [4] exist, such as the U. S. Bureau of Labor Statistics and other federal bureaus, Sales Management's *Survey of Buying Power*, studies prepared by state and municipal governments on business, business trends, population flow, movement of families, and other pertinent data. In addition, they will want to gather primary data of several kinds, to be covered fully in the chapters that follow.

Smaller stores, without research budgets, must rely on secondary sources alone. Again these include government statistics, data gathered by local business bureaus and informal surveys. Sometimes the management personnel of these retail stores of lesser sales volume feel they have more than enough to do without studying the avalanche of reports, statistics, figures that can flow across their desks. Each business must determine for itself what is needed. Generally, the more information a store has in this area of the consumer-customer the better.

What does a store want to know about the consumer? First, it should be interested in all the data available about the population of the area in which the store is located, and perhaps in several areas, if the store's branches are in non-connecting suburbs as well as in center city.

The trend of population is, in itself, important. Is this town growing or diminishing? Is this suburban area increasing or decreasing in population? (Strange as it may seem in 1974, there are areas that are losing residents.) What is the flow of residents, in or out of the area? What kind of houses exist (apartments: low, garden-type, high-rise; private homes, farms, ranches, etc.)? What is the age-spread? How many are older persons, how many in the middle years? How many youth? Children? What's the school system like? Are there colleges in the area? What about income? Professions? Job opportunities?

This is just a partial, almost superficial list of questions a store ought to ask about the consumer population in general. To a greater or lesser degree, every store can find these things out.

Then we ought to move closer to home. An established store must answer the question: What kinds of customer come to *my* store? Are the kinds diverse? Does my store satisfy (apparently) many different income groups, ages, etc.? Or, does my customer list bulk largely around one loosely defined type: middle-income, interested in value, in the accepted fashion, for example; or is my customer fashion-minded, upper income, and so forth.

How can you tell? Management can—by survey and by observation, by analysis of merchandise inventories and sales figures.

While a later chapter (Ch. 21) will cover research possibilities in detail, a comment should be made here of the SPICE [5] electronic register system, recently developed by Pitney Bowes-Alpex Inc. of Danbury, Conn. This new system, at a check-out or cash-receiving counter, scans encoded merchandise tickets, and transmits the data directly to the computer. Its importance in the promotional function of a retail store is the immediacy of its read-out, capable of producing on-the-spot reports on sales and merchandise movement.

Take a good hard look at the charge accounts. *Look at the charge accounts as people, not numbers.* Analyze purchases, changes in patterns of buying, apparent growth of families, etc. Take a sampling and follow a few families through five years. The results can be surprising, informative, and valuable.

For the Advertising Department, all the information it can gather from management's data is important for its long-range promotional plans.

In addition, the department's manager and copywriters must understand consumer buying motives, must know which of these apply to retail purchases.

Consumer motivation may be divided into three categories:

Primary motives are those which dictate the need or desire for a product type, as, "I need a new frying pan," or "I need a new raincoat."

Selective motives indicate a preference for one kind or brand over another, as, "I'd like a Teflon II ® frying pan," or, "I think I'll look for a London Fog ® coat."

Patronage motives lead to the decision to shop at one store in preference to another, whether or not a selective brand is indicated. For example, "I need a new frying pan; I'll pick one up at The Denver Store," or, "I need a new raincoat; I'll look into Mary Brown's shop and see what she has."

To some extent, each of these motivational forces must be the concern of the retail advertiser. In a narrow sense, *primary* motivation is of great concern to the national advertiser, the producer or manufacturer. This is especially true where the producer holds the major share of market: *i.e.*, where his company is the leader in sales volume in a given field. Here, the national advertiser can say, "I must stress the importance of tunafish in the weekly diet, because I know that if the housewife gets my message and buys tunafish, it is six to four she will buy my brand."

If the product is a new one in the field, the producer's advertising must motivate the consumer to try the product.

In the area of *selective* motives, the brand-name advertising can be handled most successfully at the national level, with their larger budgets and the consequent ability to stress the brand name in saturation campaigns in mass media.

The retailer, however, has two main opportunities to involve the *selective* motives. First, these come into play where he prides himself on his large assortments of well-known national brands. Then the retailer can say, "You've heard about this brand on national television or in national magazines; now buy it here; we have it." Second, *selective* motivation is an important consideration where the retailer has his *own brand,* usually tested, comparable in quality, and sometimes less expensive. Here, he must stress in his advertising that *his label* is the brand to select because of its inherent qualities. This will have to be emphasized product by product so that his store brand will be the drawing card for the purchaser.

It is to the *patronage* motive, of course, that the retailer must look for his special advertising "plus." Here, he must lay before the prospective customer every reason for shopping at his store now, today, and regularly in the future. His store, its merchandise, its assortments, its policies, services, facilities, location—all have their place here in this area in which the appeal is to the *patronage* motive.

In addition to this kind of classification, it must be realized that the consumer as an individual is complex, and the body of customers even more so.

If you are interested in advertising, you must be interested in consumer psychology. If you are in a retail store, furthermore, or in the process of seeking or getting, and then keeping, the job, you have thought about the store, analyzed its role in relation to its customers. Therefore, you must, by this time, have asked yourself the question at the beginning of these paragraphs: Who are the customers of this store? This time the answers must be psychological in their interpretation of the consumer, centered in his needs and wants, and in one additional concept, as follows.

Just as your store has its objectives set forth in its advertising plans, and you will additionally have a goal for the particular advertisement you are asked to write, so too, *the consumer has an objective*. He has a very clear objective if he has any purpose at all as he sits down to read the newspaper, the magazine, or the catalog, or to hear the broadcasts. This objective is always connected with his own inner concept of who and what he is, or of what he would like himself to be.

For our purposes, as the consumer reads or watches the media for information or entertainment, if the eye and brain pick up advertising even briefly, the hidden objective goes to work. He wants something for his money, but far deeper than that, *he wants something for his ego-concept*. This latter acts subconsciously, and is what triggers his susceptibility to advertising that "happens to reach him," that he does not consciously sit down to read or listen to.

It may be that his outward objective is to buy, for instance, a lawnmower of good quality at a good price. But far deeper than that, he wants to have the greenest, smoothest lawn on the block. He wants to keep that grass cut and thus uphold his self-image of the good householder and good neighbor. Deeper even than that, there is another goal which is a kind of self-preservation: he does not want to wear himself out each weekend. All of these are *his objectives*, conscious or not.

Thus, advertising, in its very first impact, whether of headline or artwork, must show it can fulfill the consumer's objective, conscious or hidden; while, underneath that, it must fulfill the store's and this advertisement's immediate goal, as well.

How Advertising Works

Well within the planning period, and closely allied to a discussion of the consumer, there should be some consideration of how advertising functions to accomplish these goals. How does it reach its objectives, whatever they may have been?

This can be answered in several ways; what would be appropriate for national advertising is not necessarily the same as the answer to be given for retail advertising.

All advertising accomplishes its ends by providing the consumer with (a) factual information and (b) psychological promise.

Retail advertising should fulfill the first requirement (a) by supplying whatever factual merchandise details the consumer needs to make a *rational purchasing decision*.

But we know that the consumer's ego-needs and hidden objectives must be met, too, and they must be reached by (b) psychological promise and stimulation.

A very old mnemonic, AIDA, set up four steps through which it was felt a good advertisement led a consumer. These letters stand for:

A—to attract *attention* to the advertisement
I—to gain *interest* in reading (listening) further
D—to create a *desire* to own the product
A—to lead to *action* (call, phone, write, come in, etc.).

Recent studies, however, provide somewhat more insight into this subject. These studies have been designed to turn the early inquiry (how does advertising work?) into an investigation of "how is the consumer stimulated to buy?"

New models of buying behavior have been proposed that reflect the additional probing of recent years into consumer behavior on the purchasing process. Three of these are shown against the traditional AIDA, with a fourth which this author proposes as a retail model (Fig. 6), page 54.

There is clear evidence that whichever of the newer models is examined, the consumer is viewed as having a much more intelligent and rational approach to advertising than was earlier thought to be true. Much of the new research indicates that whatever needs, wants, or desires the consumer may have and however emotionally based these may be at the early stages, there must be a *rational conviction and motivation* close to or at the time of purchase.

A retail model must, however, be set up to incorporate the pertinent step-by-step process through which the consumer moves from reading or listening to buying, and thus to becoming a customer.

The first step of some models, *unawareness*, is eliminated in the retail model, since it is only in the rarest of cases that the store can

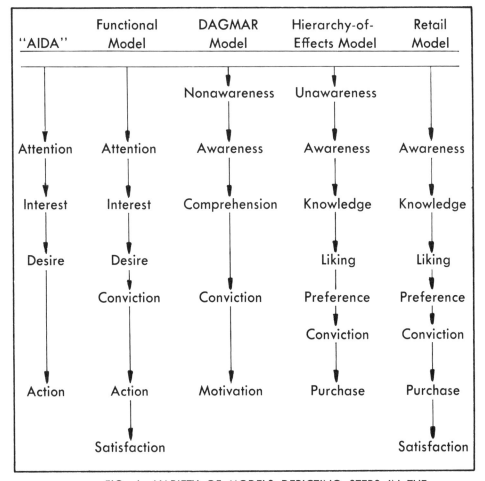

FIG. 6   VARIETY OF MODELS DEPICTING STEPS IN THE
PURCHASE PROCESS [6]

bring something to the consumer's attention of which he is really
unaware.

Our first step, then, is *awareness* that certain merchandise is
available, and that it may begin to fulfill some need. The next step
is to bring the consumer into an area of *knowledge,* with information that this store has the merchandise, and with further details
on fabrics, performances, sizes, periods—whatever is appropriate.

The steps of *liking, preference*, and then *conviction* are marks of
progress to where the advertising has *convinced* the consumer that

his own needs and goals can be met by this merchandise, these products. The next step of *purchase* is clear enough.

Again we have set up a unique retail model by addition of the final step of *satisfaction*. This step is a necessary one both for the consumer, now customer, and the store. This step really completes the process. From the customer's point of view, his satisfaction means that his goals have been fulfilled, and in a good sale, this feeling of having made a good purchase, of being a "wise shopper," should last as long as the product. For the store, satisfaction means that it has, first through its advertising and then through its personnel on the selling floor and the merchandise itself, made a consumer into a customer. The longer the feeling of satisfaction lasts, the more tightly bound is he as a loyal customer.

Media Considerations

Since three chapters will be devoted to media, the discussion here will limit itself to an overview not of how media are selected, but simply of their importance in planning.

In most cities, the retailer has his choice of a morning or an afternoon daily newspaper and one Sunday newspaper. In just a few large metropolitan areas, there are several newspapers still being published. Our cities, even the largest, have seen a sad loss of a variety of newspapers—and this despite large and devoted readership.

In some cities, there are local weeklies, such *The New Yorker* and *New York*. *The New Yorker* has achieved almost national distribution and occupies a niche of its own. In other cities (and some states) there are monthly magazines, as *Philadelphia, Connecticut Living, The Beacon* (Honolulu), and others.

Large or highly specialized stores find it advantageous to run their retail advertising in national fashion and home-service magazines, as *Vogue, Glamour, House and Garden*, and the like.

Direct mail has always been an important medium for the retailer. It should be prized especially for its personal tone in enabling the retailer to keep in touch with his charge customers. Extensions of the use of direct mail bring the retailer into the homes of prospective customers, as well.

Broadcast media, radio and television, have been added to the traditional newspaper advertising for almost all large retail stores. This is not true for smaller stores. Radio has been used for more than a generation, and ought to be a casually accepted medium for most stores. Television commercials, on the other hand, present a somewhat new medium for most retailers. Perhaps it would be wise to remark that New York City has a lot to learn from retailers in the rest of the country, many of whom are making impressive use of television. (It is, of course, acknowledged that time costs run very high in New York City, and the retailers of that city may be hard put to justify these costs and their hard-to-assess results against the more stable costs and more calculable results of news-paper advertising.)

ILLUSTRATION 2   Outdoor Advertising

Transit advertising (advertising on buses and subways, at airports, etc.) provides an opportunity for poster-like announcements for retail stores.

Outdoor advertising (see Ill. 2) shares something of the nature of transit advertising, on a much larger scale. If this medium is used at all, the sites must be selected carefully. Today, ecology and the aesthetics of an outdoor landscape are of primary concern. There is little value in a retailer's placing his advertisement where it is a blot on the horizon and an irritant to what should be his best customers. This is an important consideration and should not be overlooked. Indeed, if a retail store has heretofore used outdoor advertising, it is strongly advised that it take a good hard look at its locations and weed out those that may be offensive.

Budget Considerations

Again, we come to an area that must receive full analysis in its own chapter. Here, however, it can be quickly mentioned as an important facet of planning.

Budgeting, except in the coldest dollars-and-cents meaning of the word, is very difficult to separate absolutely from two other areas of our plan. First, it is closely linked to *objectives,* for what you want to do dictates to an extent what you need to spend (and vice versa). Second, budgeting is tied tightly to media selection. Certain media are high in cost, wherever they are located, and must be taken out of the "media mix" if the budget is small.

Methods of arriving at an appropriate figure, of allocating that overall figure to specific departments and to specific promotions, and possible ways of stretching the money available will be considered in chapters 9 and 10.

Time

When retail advertising plans are being formulated on a long-range scale, it is important to set down in the written policy statement what extent of time is meant to be covered. Plans that can extend to 1980 have been previously mentioned, and in 1973 or 1974 that new decade is not so far away. But whatever the period is, it should be clearly stated.

In the middle-range planning, it is usually the Advertising Department that stipulates the time-period for the plan. If it is customary to work on a six-month plan, then the time element is six months. If a two-month plan is the rule, then the time element is two months.

Here, too, however, the *season* and the *calendar events* (the second meaning of "time") must be given full consideration. These appear to be obvious. Christmas falling within a middle-range planning period certainly dictates the nature of the plan. So with Easter, Summer, and so forth. Because they are obvious, they may be taken for granted. But they must never be left out of the written plan. Calendar events will often furnish focal points for the middle-range plan.

In short-term planning, from week to week, the events bulk larger than the time factor. They will, of course, have already been figured into the written plan. It is clear that short-term plans must fit into the wider scope of the middle-range planning.

Responsibility

It is at the time of planning long-range policy that the placement of responsibility for overall advertising should be made. There are, as already hinted, three possibilities:

1. The Advertising Department within the store handles the entire job.
2. The advertising agency handles the entire job.
3. The Advertising Department works with an advertising agency.

The first alternative is prevalent throughout the country. In large or small stores, the Advertising Department, itself, is staffed to handle the entire advertising function of the store and its branches. As has been noted earlier, the department may be a one-man show or a 50-man department.

The second alternative exists but is not usual. An earlier discussion indicated that few advertising agencies are equipped to work at the fast pace demanded by a retail operation.

In a growing number of stores, however, the Advertising Department calls upon the services of an agency to perform any or all of the following tasks:

1. To plan and place advertising for a large promotion, such as the opening of a branch store

2. To plan and place advertising for a unusual special event, such as 100th Anniversary celebration

3. To handle its television production

4. To select and buy radio and television time

5. To work on special mailings, as: the Christmas catalog, a back-to-school brochure, and the like

6. To handle the printing and production of special advertising

7. To handle the production of regular advertising if special type faces and reproduction are required, beyond the capabilities of the local newspaper

Whatever the decision, this assignment of responsibility is part of the long-range planning. The specific assignment of tasks within the Advertising Department becomes a step in middle-range planning. The more this is done within the longer time, the less will it be necessary to "push the panic button" at short range for special jobs that may come into the department.

Evaluation

The last step in all planning ought to be a provision for judging what has been accomplished.

In the long-range plan, an evaluative technique may be set up at intervals across the year or years of the plan. In middle-range planning, the evaluation may come at the close.

The evaluation is research into how closely one's objectives have been achieved. The kind of research will depend on the kind of objectives that were originally set up. Detailed discussion of this kind of research must again be deferred until near the close of this text, where many avenues of research will be reviewed.

Perhaps it should be emphasized here, nevertheless, that unless provision is made *in the plan*, review and judgment are too often avoided altogether. Moreover, the knowledge that an evaluation will be made helps to clarify the objectives as they are set forth at the very beginning.

FOOTNOTES

[1] Colley, Russell H., *Defining Advertising Goals for Measured Advertising Results*, ANA, New York, 1969, pg. 22.

[2] Collins, Kenneth, *Successful Store Advertising*, Fairchild Publications, N.Y., 1959.

[3] Colley, op. cit., pg. 62 ff., freely adopted for "retail."

[4] Reference is made in these paragraphs to two sources of data, primary and secondary. *Primary* refers to original data-gathering conducted solely and currently for the project in hand. *Secondary* sources supply data already gathered for other organizations, other purposes, at other times. Much of this, however, may be completely pertinent to the present need. Secondary sources are always investigated first, to save time, money, and perhaps dead-end effort.

[5] SPICE is an acronym for Sales Point Information Computing Equipment.

[6] Albert Wesley Frey and Jean C. Halterman, *Advertising*, 4th ed., The Ronald Press Co., New York, 1970. Loosely adapted.

PART THREE

APPROPRIATIONS
AND MEDIA

As has been suggested in the pages on Planning Advertising Strategy (Chapter 8), it is hard to find agreement on the best order in which to present or even to think about media and budgets. In national advertising, where objectives are often intangible, perhaps the correct order of presentation is: media first, then budgets. In retail advertising, however, what we expect of advertising is much easier to define. Accordingly, we can plan in more specific terms and, in that planning, set forth budget constraints. This section, therefore, opens with a chapter on appropriations followed by a chapter on cooperative advertising opportunities. Then, a chapter covers media with its variety, availability, and strategy. Another chapter discusses programming and the buying of print and broadcast media. Finally, a last chapter in this section covers miscellaneous media used by retailing and particularly important to it.

9

APPROPRIATIONS FOR ADVERTISING

In any operating budget for a retail store there must be a line for advertising expenditures. This may appear by itself, or as a sub-line of the sales-promotion overall figure. In either case, it must, of course, be estimated as a cost of doing business.

For actual appropriation for advertising, we must move to the middle-range planning area. Generally, well in advance of a given six-month fiscal period, the management committee on sales promotion and advertising prepares its estimates for a sales-promotion appropriation. Within that planning period, the advertising manager determines the advertising appropriation, covering the necessary expenditures for the various departments of the store, as well as for the corporate or institutional advertising that the long-range planning may have dictated. How is this figure arrived at?

There are several possible approaches regularly used by retail businesses. They will be listed here roughly in order of the increased sophistication of the planning that dictates the use of one or another. It should be explained that all methods end up in some approximation of the advertising expenditure as a ratio of projected sales. The paragraphs that follow the listing will, it is hoped, explain this statement satisfactorily.

To return to the list of possible approaches to deriving an advertising budget, these include:

1. "Top-of-the-head" or arbitrary method
2. Educated "guess-timate"
3. Percentage of current or past season's sales
4. Competitive dollar-matching
5. Percentage of anticipated volume
6. "Objectives-in-perspective" approach.

Each of these methods will be described and weighed in these successive paragraphs.

1. The *arbitrary method* permits the proprietor of a retail store to make a personal, unilateral decision. (The word "proprietor" is used deliberately, since, as businesses grow beyond the smallest one-man type, it is mandatory to have the advice of an accountant, who will surely suggest other, more acceptable methods.) This method, however, is foolhardy. It takes nothing into account; it looks neither forward nor backward; and, it is hoped, starts and ends in a textbook description.

2. The second approach, *"guess-timate,"* calls for the planner to do a little figuring, a great deal of floor-pacing, to take a determined look at last season's profits and then to throw out a figure that he earnestly believes he can afford to spend on advertising, give or take two or three percent.

3. The idea of taking a *percentage* of sales is not a bad one, but unless one plans to walk backward in time, a percentage of last season's or current sales is *not* the way to do it. One of the acceptable ways *is* discussed in #5 below.

4. *Competitive dollar-matching* is only too frequently used, just as competitive merchandising and promotion-matching is too frequently the resort of the "me-too" store manager. That manager has little imagination and less initiative. What will ultimately happen is that, time and time again, competition will get the headstart —whether in merchandising or in promotion. It is no way to do business. Checking your competitor's advertising and estimating what he is spending, and then coming to a decision for your own budget ignores all the elements of advertising planning that have

already been discussed. This will be touched upon again in an analysis of #5 and #6, the only acceptable approaches to setting up an advertising appropriation.

5. By far the most popular method is that roughly described as taking a *percentage of the anticipated volume.* A check across the country indicates that stores which command national respect use this method. The stores that stand out head and shoulders above even the "good" stores combine #5 and #6, *i.e.* set up a percentage of the anticipated volume for the given period with close inspection of the objectives of the store.

6. *Objectives-in-perspective.* In looking closely at our preferred (combination) approach, we must go back to what was said earlier about advertising goals. In retail advertising, *sales can be a goal; sales are increased directly as a result of advertising.* But there are other goals and objectives, too, that retail advertising can achieve. Many of these non-sales objectives parallel the long-range plans of top management. For example, advertising can help fulfill the goals of the store within the area of community service, and help the store to take its place in the community. (This, incidentally, has become more important in the last few years and will unques-

FIG. 7   SALES VOLUME CHART SHOWING PATTERN OF GROWTH OVER 5 CONSECUTIVE YEARS

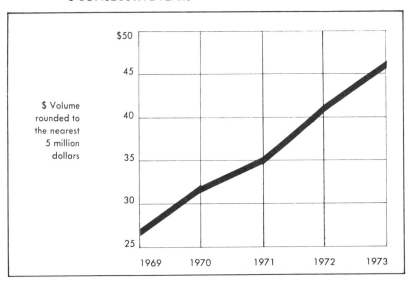

tionably increase in the coming years to a point of necessity if a store is to win and maintain the acceptance of the community and its consumer-neighbors.)

If this is so, then we must put our *objectives in perspective* and lay them out, as a sort of refining filter over the percentage-of-future-sales figures we want to use.

We should indeed start, in the most desirable approach to finding a logical appropriation figure, with a projected sales-volume figure. An advertising manager ought to have all the help he can get from the financial wizardry of the store. The comptroller (or other financial officer) should have his statistical personnel prepare a chart which shows the pattern of growth of the store in past years. (See Fig. 7.)

When this is completed, consideration should be given to some of the following, to all of them, or, in fact, to even more elements that affect future business than can be listed here:

1. The trend of the national economy
2. The trend of the local economy—How is your area doing? What are the unemployment/employment figures? Are there danger signs or hopeful signs in factories and large businesses?
3. Corporate management long-range plans
4. Trend of the population in your area
5. Population shifts
6. Municipal improvement plans
7. Competition.

Thus, with the store's own past record and a hard look at the environment, the volume for the coming fiscal period can be set up. With a realistic look at these figures of past volume and past advertising expenditures, the advertising manager can *begin* to set up his appropriation. He will take an adjusted percentage of the projected sales volume—"adjusted" to match his perspective of the objectives.

In several places in the previous paragraph, the word "percentage" has been used without any reference to *what* percentage is meant. This percentage is an arbitrary figure, arrived at over the years, and apparently accepted by and acceptable to stores throughout the country.

Generally, the percentage is set, for retailing, at from 2 to 5 percent for *all* sales promotion. Since advertising costs are usually the largest single cost of all sales-promotion activities, running between 50 percent and 60 percent, he ought to set his *advertising* percentage roughly and temporarily, at 3 percent.

If a store stops at this point, it will already have used a far more intelligent approach than is usual among most stores who, if they use method #5, simply project the sales volume and take a percentage.

Of these stores, it may be helpful to note that the smallest and the largest spend at the lower end of the percentage span, the smallest because they cannot afford to go higher, and the largest because their dollar-volume is so great that they can "make do" with the lower percentage. Medium-sized stores spend at the upper end, about 5 percent.

But the ideal appropriation figure has not yet been arrived at. Some paragraphs back, it was suggested that all the statistical work be completed and a *temporary* figure be set.

Now is the time to review long-term objectives and middle-range goals in terms of *tangibles* like sales expectations and *intangibles* like acceptance, approval, upgrading of consumer and community attitudes, and the like. It is at this point that the advertising director must ask the question: In the light of these, what must the store spend in the coming advertising period to achieve these goals? Is it a fraction more than the flat percentages? Does he have enough for his task? And, how does he know?

The answers to the first two questions must lie in the judgment-based-on-experience of that advertising director. It must rest, too, on kind and costs of the media available.

But the answer to the third question, "How does he know?" can only be answered by research. As has been indicated earlier, research must accompany—in fact, must parallel—all current advertising activities.

Thus, to sum up, the most intelligent approach to establishing an advertising appropriation for modern retailing is to start with a sophisticated projection of sales volume, take a given percentage of that figure, and finally adjust it for the objectives that the advertising plan has set forth.

Throughout this chapter so far, the word "appropriation" has been used. What of the word "budget," and the difference between the two?

The word appropriation has been reserved for the overall figure that the advertising department determines it will have to spend. After approval by management, it becomes the *budget* under which the department operates. Within the boundaries of the approved appropriation, then, we begin to slice up the money "pie." This dividing up calls for many kinds of cuts (and the pie metaphor is not at all a good one). There are at least three classifications:

1. Divisions and departments—as the budget for Better Coats; the budget for Menswear, etc.

2. Media to be used—as, the budget for newspaper linage, the budget for radio time, and so forth.

3. Short-range time periods, sometimes two-week intervals.

When these allocations have been made, the Advertising Department does, at last, have a budget. It is, as has been noted in one of the earliest chapters, the task of the Advertising Department to see that each division is furnished with a copy of its agreed-upon budget, for guidance and follow-through throughout the store.

10

COOPERATIVE ADVERTISING

Over and above its own budgeted appropriation, retail stores have an opportunity to expand their advertising dollars with some vendor dollars, too.

For retailers, cooperative advertising is the plan under which a producer, whether a fiber, textile, or manufacturing firm, undertakes to pay for some part of the advertising of the product by a retailer or distributor in regular public media (newspapers, magazines, radio, or television). The amount offered can be anything at all, usually 30 percent, 50 percent, or more. The agreement entered into usually limits itself to a specific percentage of the retailer's purchases. The portion paid by the producer varies mainly according to industry tradition. By this we mean that, for example, the girdle industry frequently pays 30 percent, while the cosmetic industry may offer closer to 100 percent.

Under a wider definition of the term "cooperative advertising," many variations of sharing the cost of an advertisement must be recognized.

There are two large classifications: vertical and horizontal cooperative advertising. The latter refers to multi-business shared advertising, where the participants are on the same promotional level. At the national level, there may be cooperation between a producer of canned fish (like tuna fish) and a producer of a mayonnaise dressing, or a cereal company and the National Dairy Association. It can cover a cooperative effort between an automobile and a dress manufacturer, or an airline and a luggage company. This is usually referred to, however, as a tie-in, not as cooperative advertising. This is basically a matter of terminology.

At the retail level, horizontal cooperative promotion or advertising can be evidenced in the dual participation of a ski shop and a resort, or an apparel store and a restaurant, and so on. Very frequently, a street of shops will advertise together. But most prominently of all, horizontal cooperation promotion is exemplified in the stores within a shopping center pooling their resources to share in advertising and promotions.

When we talk, however, of a retail store's extending its budget through cooperative advertising, we are invariably talking of the vertical type of cooperative advertising. As has been noted, this refers to the producer's or manufacturer's practice of offering his retailers a certain percentage of the cost of advertising certain products *at the retail level.*

The ramifications will be covered later. First, it should be asked: "Why do the manufacturers do this?"

A one-word answer could be given: "Exposure!"

But certainly that is not explanation enough. The *retail* advertisement, of all classifications, is the one most frequently seen, read, believed, and acted upon by the consumer. If this is so, then this is where the producer wants to be. National advertising has carried the company and product name to the consumer; now it is necessary to tell that consumer that the product is available *now, at her favorite store.* It is necessary, often, to add to the product name the glamor and reputation of the local retailer. These are the outstanding reasons, but later in the chapter, a summary of advantages will complete the coverage.

In the most frequent cases, the producer has his national campaign going, as has been suggested above. The cooperative advertising then reinforces this major campaign. On the other hand, some producers substitute a heavy cooperative venture for their own national campaign. Most successful advertising and authorities on

CO-OPERATIVE ADVERTISING PROGRAM

for jantzen sportswear and related accessories

MEN'S, BOYS', MISSES', GIRLS', TEENS' AND LABEL 4 jrs.

This cooperative advertising program for current season merchandise is offered to all regular accounts. It replaces all previous general programs on these lines and becomes effective January 1, 1971. Jantzen will not participate in the cost of advertising for closeouts or discontinued merchandise.

NEWSPAPER ADVERTISING

BASIS OF COMPENSATION

Jantzen will pay 50% of the newspaper's actual and reasonable NET charge for space, after any discounts, for advertising featuring Jantzen or Label 4 jrs. merchandise plus 50% of the newspaper's color surcharge if color is used. (Production charges are not covered.) If other color ads appear on the same page, the surcharge must be prorated.

TO QUALIFY, A NEWSPAPER AD MUST:

1. Feature Jantzen or Label 4 jr. merchandise exclusively. Jantzen merchandise must be clearly separated from other merchandise appearing on the same page. In both copy and artwork, Jantzen's portion of the ad must stand alone as a unit.

2. Prominently display the Jantzen or Label 4 jrs. name in 30 point type or larger, or in a type size not smaller than the largest type used for the store name in the ad.

3. Be a minimum of:

For Misses' or Label 4 jrs. merchandise - - - 1/2 page (full page tabloid).

(Any Jantzen merchandise including intimate apparel, may be grouped together with Jantzen Misses' or Label 4 jrs. to make up the 1/2 page minimum.)

For Men's, Boys', Girls' or Accessories - - - 1/4 page (1/2 page tabloid.)

(Men's, Boys', Teens', Girls' and Accessories may be grouped together in any combination to make 1/4 page minimum.)

4. Appear in a daily or weekly newspaper having its circulation audited by Audit Bureau of Circulation. Favorable consideration will be given to other suitable media, but prior approval must be obtained.

RADIO AND TV

Jantzen will pay 50% of the actual reasonable cost of air time for spot commercials featuring Jantzen or Label 4 jrs. merchandise. (Sponsorship of programs is not covered.)

The Jantzen or Label 4 jrs. name must be prominently mentioned. TV commercials must also include the Jantzen or Label 4 jrs. logo.

CIRCULARS, STATEMENT ENCLOSURES AND CATALOGS

Jantzen will pay 50% of the actual reasonable cost of production and printing for ads featuring Jantzen or Label 4 jrs. merchandise in these media.

The Jantzen or Label 4 jrs. name must appear in a type more prominent than the smallest type in the body copy on the same page.

LIMITATION

Jantzen's share of the cost of all advertising and advertising materials on any season's merchandise lines shall not exceed 5% of net shipments of those lines.

Exception: If shipments of the corresponding lines of the previous year were greater than in the current season, then those figures shall apply.

For purposes of determining the 5% entitlement, season's merchandise lines are defined as:

1. Spring/Summer
2. Fall/Holiday

HOW TO COLLECT FOR ADVERTISING

All claims are to be sent to:

Advertising Checking Bureau Inc.
Jantzen Section
P. O. Box 3419, Rincon Annex
San Francisco, California 94119

NEWSPAPER ADS - Send three full tear sheets and an invoice for 50% of the actual amount paid to the newspaper.

RADIO AND TV - Send the following:

a. Copy of script.
b. Copy of station's invoice for time.
c. Station's affidavit of performance.

CIRCULARS, STATEMENT ENCLOSURES, AND CATALOGS — Send the following:

a. Copy of the piece
b. Invoice for 50% of the pro-rated cost of the Jantzen space.
c. Statement indicating the number printed.

Invoices should be submitted within 60 days from date advertising is run. Payment will be made by check. Do not deduct from merchandise remittances.

OTHER ADVERTISING MATERIALS

The program covers the following list of available promotional material. 50% of the value of these items will be paid by the customer and the balance will be paid from the cooperative advertising program. Order through your sales representative or directly from Jantzen Inc., Portland, Oregon.

DISPLAY MATERIAL	VALUE
Golden Youth Awards	$ 7.00
Coloranger T-Stand Display	16.00
Gyro Seller Display	56.00
"Shop Lifter" Display	120.00
Contoured Sweater Hanger	.80
Men's 3/4 Manikin	71.00
Misses' 3/4 Manikin	50.00
Jantzen Identification Sign	2.00
Half-Shell Form	16.00
Double Take Counter Display	28.00
High — Low Display	45.00
Three Story Circle	80.00
Slack — Track Display	45.00
Two Story Display	80.00

Any customer may participate in any or all of the advertising or promotional media or materials described in this program.

Jantzen reserves the right to amend or withdraw this program at any time without notice.

ILLUSTRATION 3   Cooperative Advertising

advertising theory do not support this strategy; it must be admitted that the sales managers of manufacturers are usually the most vocal in support of what is basically a short-sighted policy. (In a text on advertising management, your author would have some comments on that practice. In this book on *retail advertising*, any further discussion would be out of place.)

What are the advantages to the retailer? Clearly, the big factor to a retailer is to augment his advertising budget with vendor funds. In addition, the gain to any store in linking its name with a powerful, well-advertised national name or brand is great. The potential for sales is increased, as well, when a store advertises its own name with that of any popular brand, of whatever size. The retail advertising, taking advantage of the large national campaign, can say to the local customer: "You have been seeing this name in your favorite magazine. Now you can buy it here!"

Just as frequently, less widely advertised national names that carry perhaps the prestige of fashion leadership or fine design in furniture, china, glassware, and so on, will add to a store's reputation. The very fact of the store's carrying this or that carefully designed line, however limited in actual sales its price may make it, helps the store promote its own prestige.

Furthermore, the additional advertising dollars can be used to gain greater frequency of advertising, to explore new media, and to support basic budgets, which in themselves may be generous (or is there ever enough?).

In any case, the terms under which the producer or manufacturer agrees to reimburse a store, and the store agrees to advertise with the producer, must be spelled out in a contract. These vary considerably. Some are legalistic and complicated. Other are simple. One of the clearer contracts is included here in Ill. 3 on page 70.

In most stores, the buyer or merchandise manager accepts or approves and signs the contract for the store. Certainly, in all the stores, the buyer gets the contract, usually from the supplier's salesman. In too few retail stores (but these few are among the better administered), the cooperative advertising agreement or contract must be channeled to the advertising manager or sales-promotion manager for further approval and counter signature.

It is, of course, eminently reasonable that the merchandise manager know of any agreement to approve the buying of a certain quantity of the goods, and to agree that his store will receive a certain reimbursement upon advertising. A commitment has thereby been made to promote a given line.

It is even more reasonable that the advertising manager be fully aware of, and responsible for (through signature), such a commitment. The advertising manager must have this information so that he can include it in his plans and calculations. He must be aware of the possibility of the influx of funds and of certain rules laid down by the manufacturer as to how to advertise his product so that the store can get that advertising allowance.

Now that the problem has been brought squarely into the Advertising Department's bailiwick, let us examine it closely.

1.   The buyer or merchandise manager has made or is about to make a commitment to buy certain products and have the store promote and advertise them.

2.   The manufacturer or producer of that product undertakes to reimburse the store a certain percentage of the store's cost of the advertisement, usually requiring that the advertising be done in a certain way, or contain certain specific elements.

3.   If the store has set up its guidelines properly, the merchandise manager has time to decide if his buyer is making a wise decision, and the advertising manager has time to review the contract demands to determine if store policy permits him to accept the manufacturer's requirements. If not, he will see if he can persuade the manufacturer that his purpose will best be served if the store advertises *his* product *in its own way*.

This can be so delicate an area of demands and pressures that federal legislation under the Robinson-Patman Act regulates how a manufacturer may set up his cooperative advertising plans. Briefly, the Robinson-Patman Act stipulates that any promotional concession offered to one retailer in a marketing area must be offered to all on a proportionate basis.

As an example: Ace Sportswear Co., Inc., offers to share 50 percent in the cost of advertising any portion of its current line, having its eye on a large city store whose initial order comes to three or five thousand pieces and which may run thousand-line advertisements for Ace Sportswear in a powerful big-city newspaper. At the same time, at the edge of town, a mom-and-pop shop may place a small order for perhaps two or three numbers, five different sizes in each, and in two or three colors—perhaps four or five dozen in all. Their channel of advertising is possibly the local shoppers' news. Ace Sportswear may have misgivings about the value of the small store's advertising to its own national objectives, but each of these stores must be handled on the same proportionate basis. So our mom-and-pop shop can look forward to receiving 50 percent payment of the cost of advertising in the little shoppers' news, upon satisfaction of any advertising requirements in the Ace agreement, and upon furnishing a tearsheet as proof of advertising.

Whether or not Ace wishes to offer this money to a small store, it is bound to do so by the Robinson-Patman Act. The sum may be very small, but it is almost always an annoyance to a producer or manufacturer. The accounting cost is the same for $50 as for $500; the frittering away of small sums will vitiate the hoped-for results of the strong promotional tool.

The Robinson-Patman Act stands firm, however, and the retailer is protected.

The retailer, who has the legal advantage, has but to make use of the allowance. First, the buyer, the merchandise manager and the advertising manager should all be aware of whatever they have agreed to do in the contractual agreement. From the retailer's advertising point of view, this should have clearly stated what the national advertising requires the retail advertiser to do. These requirements may call for the total reproduction of copy, artwork, and national logotype (sent to the store by the manufacturer, usually in the form of a complete mat). This is not usually a firm, unelastic requirement; however, if it is, then the national manufacturer is basically asking the retailers to follow what he has in mind, and sometimes what his campaign has been saying in attional magazines.

More frequently, the agreement requires the use of the manufacturer's logotype. Other manufacturers require the use of their names in a headline, in any type-form the retailer prefers. Still others require only that the name be used *any* way the retailer finds acceptable. It may be carried well within the copy body, with no special emphasis. This last method is very frequently the custom when the cooperative advertising is undertaken by the more prominent stores of the country.

In order to receive payment of the proper share of a newspaper or magazine advertisement, the retailer is expected to furnish a tearsheet of this advertisement as proof of performance. A "tearsheet" is exactly what the name implies, a printed page torn from the newspaper or magazine. The entire page is used, not just a cut-out portion of an advertisement that may be less than full-page size.

This tearsheet is sent to the manufacturer or to his designated representative with an invoice showing the total cost of the space to the retailer, the percentage agreed upon to be paid by the manufacturer, and the consequent dollar-figure the manufacturer should remit.

In radio and television, a proof of performance lies in an affidavit from the station, and a periodic aircheck. For outdoor advertising, if used for cooperative purposes, a photograph and affidavit of posting are acceptable.

The manufacturer should then send his check to the store. Remittance should *not* be made by crediting a sum against merchandise orders past or future. The buying of goods should stand on its own. Vendor advertising allowance should not be applied to goods, but should remain as an extension to the buyer's budget for advertising and promoting the merchandise.

So we have two parties agreeing to a contract, one party carrying out its requirements and furnishing proof that he has done so, whereupon the other party pays his promised share.

Early in the chapter, we discussed the manufacturer's goals in offering an advertising allowance. Since our concern, however, is with the retailer, we would like, at the cost of repetition, to review the advantages to the retailer of entering into agreements for cooperative advertising or vendor allowances:

1. The provision of extra advertising dollars.
2. The freeing of budgeted funds to increase the total ad-

vertising plan in depth; to increase frequency, to open new media, and so forth.

3. The linking of small stores' names with big-name brands, and of well-known stores' names with prestigious national names, such as those of designers, custom furnishings, etc. The gains here are in volume, patronage, and prestige.

If sensible rules are observed, there would appear to be clear sailing. If both parties stand to gain, why is cooperative advertising so controversial a subject?

Why is it a subject of interest when a manufacturer declares his company will no longer offer advertising allowances? Why did his company come to such a decision? Why does a retail advertising manager declare his store will reject all vendor-paid advertising offers?

The answers all lie in the abuses of the agreements by either side from time to time.

On the manufacturer's side, his demands may call for buying goods not really current or desirable. He may demand buying in quantities beyond what the store can use. He may make unreasonable demands on the use of *his* artwork, *his* name, adherence to *his* national campaign.

Of course, the buyer must be on the alert to buy only what his department can sell, both in type and in quantity of merchandise.

Further, because of the requirements of the Robinson-Patman Act, the manufacturer may feel, as previously suggested, that he is not spending his advertising dollars to best advantage in smaller stores which, with the best will in world, perhaps because of location or population area, cannot set out a strong or compelling campaign. Textile companies, in particular, have, in many instances, elected to eliminate retail advertising allowances entirely rather than be forced by the legislation to allocate their funds proportionately across the country.

Moreover, the requirements of the manufacturer may be so extreme as to demand of the retailer that he lose his own identity in the presentation of the brand-name, logo, type-face, and sometimes even product-artwork.

To quote one authority, ". . . the retailer should think of the 50% he spends on cooperative advertising as well as the 50% he 'saves'." [1]

On the other hand, a smaller retailer in a small town may welcome not only the advertising dollars, but the actual advertising material that many manufacturers send out under their cooperative advertising program. These are traditionally *mats,* but more recently, *plastics,* which are, respectively, pressed cardboard or plastic molds that can be used by any press, usually a newspaper, to prepare a stereotype to be used in the printing of an advertisement. At best, these present a level of professionalism in copy concept, artwork, and typography that may not otherwise be available or affordable to the small store. At worst, they are worthy of the nearest wastebasket.

The retailer must, under all circumstances, maintain his identity and the local appeal of his advertising. He must not allow his advertising space to take on the appearance of a combat area, with several national competitors fighting on the page.

The retailer, large or small, who accepts a cooperative advertising agreement ought to accept certain responsibilities for fair handling.

1. All "grey areas" of compliance ought to be spelled out and settled *before* signature is put on the contract. A buyer ought not to agree to any commitment for the use of certain copy, art, even logotype; rather, this should be the Advertising Director's prerogative, and should be referred to him—again *before* signing.

This seems to be logical, so logical that the reader may ask why it needs to be put down here. Why indeed? So simple a step is too often overlooked by the buyer in an honest endeavor to get as much money as possible for promotion. But like crabgrass or sin, it will rear its ugly head at the worst possible time—when the advertisement is about to be written and placed in the newspaper. Again, anything questionable should be ironed out before the agreement has been made firm.

2. The Advertising Department should be made aware of what is being agreed to and should at least initial the agreement, as evidence of having seen and approved it.

3.   Thereupon when the merchandise is presented to the Advertising Department with the usual "Request for Advertising," there should be no difficulty in fulfilling already accepted requirements.

4.   The Advertising Department should be prepared to furnish the manufacturer the tearsheet and an honest invoice, fairly apportioned for the vendor's share. What is an honest invoice?

Rate: Local media, specifically newspapers, have traditionally set up one rate for the national advertiser and a second, lower, rate for local companies. There are two reasons for this tradition. First, it was thought that the local advertiser would almost automatically use more space than out-of-towners, and thus the lower rate contains a built-in discount for quantity linage. Second, there was a real interest in promoting business for each other in earlier days. Now, published rates are *national* rates. Local rates are "arranged."

National advertisers expect a retail store to bill them at the same rate at which the store is billed—local (lower) linage rates. Too often, retailers do not. They bill the manufacturer at the higher national rate. The manufacturer has no accurate way of checking on each store's rates.

When a retailer bills at the higher rate, he is breaking his part of the agreement and is acting unethically.

Portion of advertisements charged: There is some real question as to what a manufacturer should pay for.

Again, here there can be real friction. In a single item advertisement of the manufacturer's product, should he be asked to pay for a portion of or the whole advertisement? Should the store subtract space areas used for its own logotype, address, store hours? Or, if the copy for one manufacturer's product is set in an assortment advertisement with, let us say, three other products of similar merchandise, should the manufacturer in question be charged for one-quarter of the total space of the whole advertisement? Or, should he be charged for the precisely measured space that his product (artwork and copy) occupies on the page?

Here, too, some policy must be set up. This is not so much a matter of ethics as of actual understanding and acceptance of prearranged agreements.

Production: Should the manufacturer be charged for the appropriate portion of the space cost only? Or should he be charged for space plus a portion of the costs of producing the advertising, artwork, typography, engraving, as well? Here, too, early agreement will save hard feelings later.

Before leaving this subject, some word should be said about other advertising and promotional materials that a manufacturer can supply to the retailer. These are often called "dealer aids," but a full recital of them will prove them broader than that term implies.

If a store uses television advertising, many large manufacturers can supply footage, frequently called "wild footage," which is actually extra seconds of action completed when their own national commercials were being shot. A retail store need add only a last frame (a "local tag") of its own name and address, to gain a highly desirable commercial for itself. The quality of the film or tape is usually high, action-packed, and dramatic. Certainly this is valuable to a store.

Other manufacturers supply radio tapes, again needing only a local tag to make them the store's own.

In other areas of promotion, manufacturers supply posters, counter cards, display stands, suggestions for window displays and for fashion shows. Publicity plans are prepared, and local releases mimeographed for the store to send to its own newspapers and radio stations. The store has only to make a decision as to what is appropriate and in keeping with its own identity.

Obviously, despite all the pitfalls, cooperative advertising of one kind or another is useful to both sides. It would seem, therefore, that the retailer ought to be able to take intelligent and ethical advantages and make sound promotional capital out of this extension of his advertising appropriation.

FOOTNOTES

1 Davidson and Doody, *Retailing Management.* 3rd ed. The Ronald Press, New York, pg. 634.

11

MEDIA OPPORTUNITIES

The choice of the medium, the channel through which the store gets its message over to its customers, whether current or potential, is so closely knit to the budget availability that its sequence in this book is almost automatic. Realistically, and this has been touched upon before, somehow or other a business ought to know what its plans are and how its objectives shape its need for a certain appropriation. But very tight on the heels of this kind of consideration is the actual dollars-and-cents cost of the media through which the store hopes to achieve its objectives. Newspaper space costs money, radio time costs money, and television time costs even more.

Thus, while objectives and plans shape the overall round figure appropriation, *the actual working budget* is arrived at after a thorough inspection of the media that are available and advisable for a store to use.

Consequently, we will enter the subject of media by taking a close look at what exists for the retailer.

The scope of media possibilities for retail advertising is limited only by the capability of the store's advertising personnel and by the advertising appropriation itself. All the channels of communication available to any advertiser are also open to the retailer.

First, let us review all the possible media that can carry a message for the retail store. They include:

1. Print, newspapers and magazines
2. Electronic or broadcast: radio, television, in-store public-address system, closed-circuit TV
3. Direct: direct advertising within the store, direct mail
4. Outdoor: billboards, posters, spectaculars
5. Transit: trains, buses, stations
6. The store itself.

Not all six are generally considered in textbooks or discussions. In fact, it is only those that are paid for *as media* that are included. But this text will cover the public-address (P.A.) system, closed-circuit TV, direct advertising, and the store itself in a later discussion of miscellaneous media. The word "miscellaneous" doesn't imply "less important." On the contrary, these are of great importance to the retail advertiser, and will become increasingly important in the future.

Newspapers

The big category in print media for retailers over the years has been the local newspaper. There are over 1500 daily newspapers, almost 10,000 weeklies, and 500 Sunday papers. These are all "measured" media, meaning that they regularly submit to an audit of their circulation by an external organization, the Audit Bureau of Checking (ABC).

In addition to these newspapers, there are free, giveaway newspapers distributed within narrow areas of neighborhoods. They are often called shopping guides, shoppers, shoppers news, or pennysavers. They carry local advertising of large and small stores, and chatty, newsy "personal" items, that are often publicity columns under a thin disguise.

The newspaper continues to carry a large bulk of the advertising messages of a store. This is entirely understandable, since the newspaper is timely, current, and local, all of which match the needs of a good retail store. Moreover, the readers rely on it and believe it to be the most helpful of all media in providing shopping information. (See Fig. 8a–b.) Some studies [1] and their results are given here, to indicate the faith that shoppers place in their newspapers.

The newspaper is a flexible medium in many ways. It permits change of individual advertisement size. Through a change in size or linage, an advertisement's shape need not be static. Thus, an advertisement can be adapted daily to the requirements of the store. Total daily linage for a store, too, need not be the same, day after day, but can be stretched or shrunk to whatever area the store requires.

In changing the combined height and width of an advertisement and thus its shape, the advertisement can suit the merchandise or products being promoted. Bedding and furnishings may call for a layout that stretches all the way across the page, but uses just the bottom half. Shoes may call for the same linage, but may be more effectively shown in a narrow, vertical layout.

Production time, too, is very short in newspapers. It is possible (though not desirable) to set an advertisement overnight. Still, it can be done if emergency dictates. It is certainly possible and feasible to set in a price or to change a price on short notice. Supermarkets do this regularly: they need this kind of flexibility.

(Additional aspects of production, such as use of color in newsprint and the like, will have to await the chapter on "Print Production" later in the text.)

Newspapers, local as they are, reflect the characteristics of their readers and thus provide an appropriate showcase for the products of the retail store that services the *locale*.

Studies recently compiled by the Bureau of Advertising (ANPA) show that people under 30 do read the newspapers, but they increase their reading as they gain increased responsibilities in their home life, on the job, and in their communities. This is important to the retail advertiser.

After 30, the young married couple, the householders, are the ones who need most of the household goods: furnishings, appliances, clothing for growing children, and so on. A high level of buying is maintained into later life, the 40's and 50's, by those whose life styles have accustomed them to possessions, and whose careers and income permit them to indulge their desire for the

FIG. 8   CUSTOMER'S RATINGS OF CONFIDENCE IN MEDIA

Question: "Suppose one of your local stores was using these kinds of advertising (television, radio, newspaper, magazines, mail circulars) for (name specified items) which one of these do you think would give you the best, most helpful information about . . . .?"

(Women were asked which of five advertising media—newspapers, radio, television, magazines, or mail circulars—would provide the best, most helpful information about three items. For each item they were asked to rate each medium for advertising information on such factors as type of material, size, price, brand, style, shape, color, etc. The items specified were a good skillet, a man's white dress shirt, and a woman's better coat.

On an overall basis, housewives preferred newspapers ten to one over other media. Seventy-eight per cent of the ratings as "best" medium to provide helpful shopping information went to newspapers. Magazines, mail circulars, and television received 7%, 8%, and 5%, respectively.

Although the runner-up varied for each of the three rated items, newspapers received by far the highest rating in all three cases.

Product	Prefer Newspapers (in %)	Rate and Medium Next Most Helpful (in %)
A Man's White Dress Shirt		
Size range, brand	77	8 (Mail Circulars)
Price	82	7 (Mail Circulars)
A Woman's Better Coat		
Style, Color, Size range	72	14 (Magazines)
Price	81	8 (Magazines)
A Good Skillet		
Shape, Material, Size	58	19 (Television)
Price	70	11 (Television)

Base: 605 total respondents

Source: Bureau of Advertising, ANPA

Product	Tele-vision	Radio	News-papers	Maga-zines	Mail Circulars	Don't Know	Total Respondents *
Media Rated Best For Advertising Specific Points Of Information About Specified Items (in %)							
A Good Skillet							
Shape	23	fr.	54	10	12	1	100%
Type of material	16	1	59	12	12	1	100% (sic)
Size	17	fr.	61	9	12	1	100%
Price	11	fr.	70	6	12	1	100%
Man's White Dress Shirt							
Size Range	6	fr.	79	6	8	1	100%
Brand	8	1	75	9	7	1	100% (sic)
Price	5	1	82	4	7	1	100%
A Better Coat							
Style	9	—	69	15	6	1	100%
Color	7	—	68	16	8	1	100%
Size Range	4	—	77	10	8	1	100%
Type of Material	5	—	73	14	8	1	100% (sic)
Price	3	—	81	8	7	1	100%

* Base: 605 total respondants
fr. = less than 0.5%

newer, the more efficient, the "status" purchase. This class has always read the newspapers, and is continuing to do so.

But it cannot be denied that all our habits are changing; our reading habits, too, are tending to slip a little before the broadcast media.

Magazines

Magazines, as a group, are a less important medium for most retailers. A special kind of retail store, whether department or specialty, with a special kind of clientele, however, may seek those customers through magazine advertising. Again, we must look at the current trend. While there are still a few general-interest magazines, the trend today is clearly toward *special-interest* publications. These are monthly or weekly publications which appeal to a part of the consumer public in small segments, and in special compartments of their lives. *Sports Illustrated,* for example, takes the otherwise general reader and focuses his attention on one aspect of his own sphere of concern: sports. Another day, the same man may pick up *Playboy* and a different part of his attention is captured by that magazine.

Similarly, a woman may read *House & Garden, Vogue, Parents' Magazine,* or *Gourmet* at different times of the day. For each reading, she turns a different side of her intelligence to bear on what she is reading. She becomes, in turn, a decorator, a stylist, a mother, a French chef, as she bends her interest to that of the publication that engages her attention at that moment.

Thus, a retail store that has built a reputation for fashion leadership may certainly find an alert audience in the readers of *Vogue* or *Harper's Bazaar.* A store with young fashions may advertise in *Seventeen,* and so forth.

This, then, begins to outline what magazine advertising brings to the store. First, through the special-interest publications, a store literally selects an audience. Generally, the audience is smaller than that of any city newspaper. Yet its members are valuable because, as just described, they are willing to listen. They have tuned in their minds and are alert and receptive to what you are saying, to your communication. Your goal may be to gain attention, to keep your name in front of a group, to remind them to stock up, to get real sales action, or any of the other feasible goals of advertising covered in a previous chapter. In a special-interest magazine, whatever your intent, you have potential readership whose eyes can be open to your message. How to build an advertisement that gains this open-eyed attention and interest is the core of what we want to arrive at, throughout this entire book.

Second, magazines, by their very nature, receive unhurried, even slow, readership and have a long life. This medium does not present the "here today, gone tomorrow" aspects of a newspaper. Of all the media, magazines have the longest life. Consequently, they ought to carry advertising that is at once current yet long-lived; a best-seller, yet at least in stock for a season. The merchandise should not be staples, but either a classic or, even better, a "one-of-a-kind" so intriguing that it brings the reader into the store with the intention of looking through everything else in the department.

In the non-fashion fields, the life of a magazine is even longer. Some stories go the rounds of advertisements that have kept pulling literally for years, until the advertiser has wondered how to turn off the responses. Every retail store can show case histories of the unbelievable longevity of a magazine advertisement.

Third, with few exceptions, the magazine page presents an attractive setting for your message. The stock (the paper on which the copy is printed) is very descriptively called "slick." It is usually

ILLUSTRATION 4   Small Space "Ads" and Stores that
Rely on Them

reasonably heavy and has a glossy coating. The reproduction of photography or illustrations is excellent. Photographs of great depth and sketches of the finest ink techniques come out on the printed page intact.

Finally, magazines provide a trustworthy directory for mail-order advertising. Many retail businesses across the country, *with or without a local store*, maintain a busy traffic with many or all of their customers by magazine advertising alone. Stores in small towns in Florida, in Massachusetts, in Georgia, for example, present fashionable or unique merchandise (clothing, furniture, toys, in fact, everything) in small space advertising. Year after year, season after season, the orders come in from all over the country. (See Ill. 4.) People believe in their favorite magazine.

With all these advantages, then, what is entailed for the retail store that plans to include magazines in its media mix? It requires several elements.

First, the merchandise manager or buyer must plan the merchandise carefully. Guided by the Advertising Department, he must plan with a good knowledge of the readership his advertisement will find. He must plan four, five, even six months ahead, since many magazines require plates two to three months in advance. Thus, taking time for choosing the merchandise, having the copy written, the artwork completed, the total advertisement engraved, you have an additional length of time that must be allowed for.

Second, the planning should be such as to take advantage of the long life of the magazine, if actual sales are a factor and an objective of the advertisement. The more sophisticated the magazine, the more knowledgeable the readers and the less likely are they to expect merchandise in a store six months after publication. In homier, more rural, less urbane books, the expectation may be that, once advertised, the merchandise *is* available whenever the customer decides to place her order.

Third, and still in the merchandising sphere of interest in such advertising, absolute assurance ought to be the rule that the merchandise *is in stock when the magazine appears,* carrying the advertisement. More goodwill is lost than can be calculated when a reader finds that the store placing the advertisement cannot deliver the goods. The buyer must have firm commitments with the manufacturer to deliver on time, in quantities and varieties of color, style, and so forth, as advertised.

In addition to this area of consideration, the preparation of the advertisement is usually more complex. Therefore, for this kind of promotion, a store may very well use an advertising agency. Photographs or sketches must be carefully prepared, mechanicals must be accurate. A high level of taste and distinction must be met and maintained. Above all, while all of these can be handled by the store's advertising department, the magazine schedules sometime are planned over and above the daily newspaper advertising and place an additional burden on an already harried department. For all of these reasons, it is sometimes felt that only an agency can satisfactorily initiate and handle all the steps necessary to production of magazine advertising.

Broadcast Media

Increasingly, retailers find broadcasting an effective advertising medium. Stores have used radio for a generation. In talking of television, perhaps it would be wise to say that our retail stores have been *experimenting* with TV for about ten years and are still experimenting. Only a small proportion can be said to use this medium regularly or effectively.

But to discuss radio first: Stores have learned how to prepare commercials, how to establish and maintain their own identity in this medium over the years. Those who have done the most effective job have understood the nature of radio's popularity. It is a very personal medium. Often, in a family, each member will have his own radio. Sometimes, they are all going at once, in different parts of the house, tuned in to different, favorite programs.

In every city, there are many radio stations, covering more or less the same geographical territory, but commanding very distinct and different audiences.

Sometimes we characterize radio stations by names that indicate the nature of their major programming. Among these are:

1. All News
2. Talk Shows
3. Classical Music

4. R&B—Rhythm and Blues
5. R&R—Rock 'n Roll
6. Ethnic
7. Foreign Language

A store's advertising manager must know what stations are available in his own city, and how his own store's customers or potential customers match these options. He will have radio maps on hand to give him information on the reach of the radio signal.

The differences between FM and AM radio are important to the retail advertiser, not necessarily in terms of mechanical or electronic characteristics, but insofar as the programming and audience profiles are different.

FM stations, with very few exceptions, are programmed for young people from early teens to mid-20's. Those "older folks" who tune in are generally those who identify closely with the life style of the young. Often FM stations present definite points of view on domestic and foreign affairs that may seem radical to some.

This is unlike most AM radio stations, whose policy it is to present an objective face to the listener. The "radicalism" of the FM stations is, of course, exactly what contributes to their popularity with the youth segment of the market. In summary, they may, to an extent, be compared to the "underground press."

Accordingly, a retail advertising manager must study each FM station thoroughly, must listen for himself before he can decide whether or not his store management will be happy with representation on these generally more-than-liberal stations.

Television stations pose no such problem for the prospective advertiser. There are few of them in each metropolitan area. In some small cities, there may be no local television station at all, although today some television signal reaches almost every city and town in the country. Television sets are said to be in 99 percent of the homes in America.[2] Particularly with cable television to boost the signal up and over the mountains in the West, more places can be reached by television than was possible five or ten years ago.

The maps reproduced here (Ills. 5 and 6) show how stations measure areas of reception and, consequently, of influence. The core area nearest the center receives the strongest signal; it is also

ILLUSTRATION 5   Radio Coverage Map

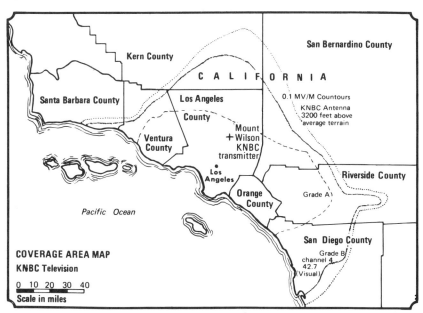

ILLUSTRATION 6   Television Coverage Map

the area where the station exerts its strongest influence in relation to programs tuned in, and commercials received and acted upon. Next is an area of diminished reception, and of lessened viewing (for TV). Finally, the outermost area receives the weakest signal where the influence of stations, too, is least.

Frequently, the last area of one station may be the core of another station's signal beam (especially is this true of radio).

Perhaps most important of all the information supplied by both radio and television stations is the demographic profile of the stations. Demographics are simply "people-facts." Each station is continually engaged, through its own research department or through outside studies, in analyzing the kinds and numbers of people who listen to that particular station.

The studies include differences in age, sex, income, education, job, status of head of family, number in family, geographic locations, and so forth. One independent research company provides 31 [3] categories in its analysis of station listeners and viewers.

These are interpreted as *quantitative* analyses which provide information on *how many* people are listening (and of what age, sex, income, etc.)—and at what hours they listen. Another research service provides a quarter-hour breakdown of such data.[4]

The advantages of using radio for retail advertising lie in the immediacy of radio programming and in its personal appeal to the listener. Radio commercials can be prepared quickly (if all other elements are present) and can be on the air within the hour if necessary. This is certainly *not recommended*. It may occur for a *change* in copy but should be only a theoretical possibility for *new* copy. Nonetheless, radio commercials, if they are to be delivered live, are fast.

They are fluid in that, when you stop broadcasting, your message disappears. Thus it is important to have a clear, easily memorable announcement. (To be covered in the next section.)

Finally, radio is an inexpensive medium. While it is possible to spend lots of money on radio commercials, it is not necessary to do so to be effective. It is certainly not desirable at all for the retailer. It is to his distinct advantage to have this fast medium in his media mix, to use it for news, something today, something else tomorrow, and so on.

Television, not yet a comfortable medium for retailers to handle, *requires* the services of a skilled professional. Consequently, the retailers who are doing the best job on television have either settled into a working arrangement with an advertising agency, or have built their own, separate TV advertising department parallel to the older, traditional print advertising department. Sears has been a leader in the steady, knowledgeable use of television as a medium of advertising, and they have established a department under a vice-president to handle the work.

It should be stated, of course, that except in rare instances (and Sears would be one of these exceptions), the retailer uses local television (as opposed to network or national TV). Retailing, no matter how many branches of a store may exist, is a local business and should communicate locally with its hometown customers.

The advantages of using television are clear. TV provides a vehicle for a *moving*, real-action advertisement. It is, of course, *advertising*, but borrows from its fellow activity, the *fashion show*. It presents apparel on real people. In house furnishings, it shows real merchandise in real-house situations, in appropriate interior designs. In appliances it *demonstrates*. Of all the things that TV can do for an advertiser, the thing it does uniquely and does best is to *demonstrate* his merchandise. Whether it be a dishwasher appliance rushing through its cycles, or a chiffon ballgown rippling in a man-made breeze, TV demonstrates how things look and act, and how people react to them.

When color is used, as it most often is now, another dimension is added, and the sense of reality is heightened.

Further, despite all the criticism of TV commercials, especially from young people, it is perhaps the boastful national commercials, not the local retail commercials, to which objection is made. The retail commercial can do exactly what we have earlier said advertising must do: provide full and correct information to help the consumer come to an intelligent decision.

With all of this going for TV, why are stores such "reluctant dragons" in the use of television? Perhaps it is because the two big demands of TV would frighten any dragon. These are:

    1.   The demand for expertise, know-how.

2. The demand on the store's budget, stemming from production costs as well as time costs.

To take the second first, the production can be handled to make costs more sensible. This area will be covered in a later section in full detail. The time costs will be treated in the next chapter.

However, to return to the demand for expertise: This is real, and the wise retail advertiser recognizes it. But, on every front, it is a diminishing problem. First, the stores themselves are moving toward TV, warily but steadily. Second, the current generation of advertising personnel, copywriters, artists, and managers too, have been accustomed to TV from their own childhood forward. They are familiar with its idiom, and desperately anxious to wet their feet in this particular area. Third, insofar as training, whether in college or on the job, contributes its share of manpower, this preliminary effort includes radio and television courses. Finally, there are innumerable advertising agencies in every metropolis in the country which are thoroughly familiar with television as a medium of advertising. They can be (and some already are) helpful to retail advertisers in the preparation of commercials with good selling power. They can be of real assistance, too, in the task of keeping costs down. As retail stores learn how it is done, their own departments may wish to take over. This is being done increasingly all across the country.

FOOTNOTES

[1] Bureau Of Advertising, ANPA, 1968.
[2] A. C. Nielsen and Company.
[3] Nielsen Studies.
[4] Pulse.

12

BUYING PUBLIC MEDIA:
SCHEDULING AND PROGRAMMING

Having made a survey of media opportunities for the retail advertiser, it is time now to see how space and time are bought and used.

The retail advertiser, who is mainly a local advertiser, is able to buy local newspaper space at lower prices than are quoted to national advertisers. There is indication that some stores are pressing for lower local rates on radio and television, too. Thus, this kind of double-billing, referred to in the chapter on Cooperative Advertising, becomes an important part of the buying and scheduling for the local store.

Newspapers

Linage in newspapers is sold by the agate line or by the column inch. An agate line (a name which is a legacy of old printing measures) is 1/14th of an inch in a top-to-bottom measurement. (See Fig. 9.) Thus 14 lines (the "agate" is usually dropped in daily usage) equals one inch. This measurement, it should be repeated, is a traditional one and bears no reference to a line of printed type one sees in the newspaper.

The "columns" refer to the division of the newspaper by vertical

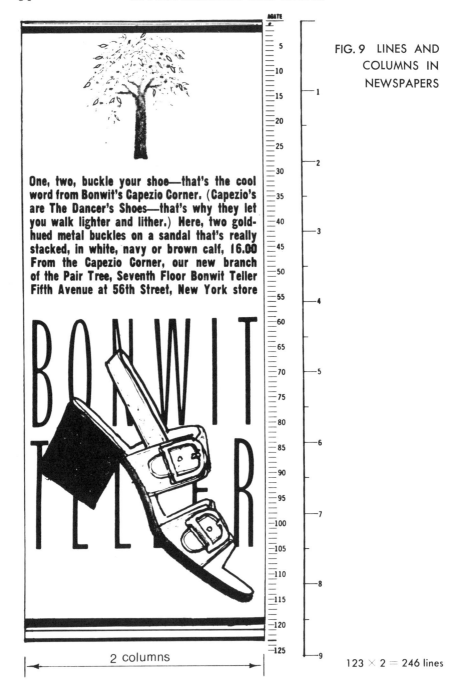

FIG. 9 LINES AND
COLUMNS IN
NEWSPAPERS

123 × 2 = 246 lines

lines or spaces. The width of a column is *never* a factor in the measurement of an advertisement for figuring cost. Whatever width a given newspaper has assigned to its columns is "what it is." Only the art and production departments are concerned so that the layouts can be made to the proper dimensions.

To those who deal with advertising regularly, like retail stores, it is customary to enter into a year's contract. The agreement provides for the maximum number of lines that a store expects to use in a year, at the lowest possible discounted cost per line. This line-rate figure can range from a few cents a line for a country newspaper to $3 and $4 a line for the large metropolitan dailies.

There is always an increasing discount for increasing use of more and more lines. Thus, if a store is large enough to contract for the maximum linage at which a maximum discount is given, it will, of course, do so.

Should a store contract for more linage (space) than it eventually uses, the publication will "short-rate" the store; *i.e.,* it will, at the end of the contract year, charge as much more per line as is necessary to bring the rate back up to the lesser discount earned for less linage.

Where the linage used is close to the contract amount, it often pays a store to run a few "rate-holders" just to bring their usage into the needed bracket. A rate-holder is a small, minimum-space advertisement run to maintain a low line rate.

Should a store underestimate its year's usage, and find itself using more linage than expected, the newspaper will credit them with a rebate to bring the line rate down to where the larger discount would have automatically set it.

While this procedure is explained here under "Newspapers," exactly the same procedure is followed wherever similar discount-policies obtain, principally in radio and television, covering time contracted for (instead of space). In magazines, a "frequency" discount may be given instead of one for multiple pages. However, both are to be found.

(Since the usage of magazines by retail stores is generally limited, the question of maximum space or frequency, and subsequent contract discounts, can be passed over here. Those stores which *do* use the medium regularly will certainly take advantage of any and all discounts available.)

In many cities, an evening (afternoon) newspaper will be affiliated with a morning paper. Either or both may publish a Sunday edition, as well. Various combination rates are available to advertisers.

The best source of this kind of information is, of course, the newspaper itself, although another source will be cited later. A telephone call will bring a representative to your desk, with all the information you will need, and a rate card to be kept and referred to as often as necessary.

Color is available today. It is not universal, however, but can be found mainly in our largest cities. More than one type of color printing is offered across the country. That does not mean that retailers in a given city have a choice. In the very largest cities, among the top fifty markets, SpectaColor may be offered. This is a pre-printed section run in a roll with, of course, bright color inks. The paper itself is a semi-gloss stock. This process is used more frequently by national food advertisers than it is by national apparel or local retail advertisers.

R.O.P. (run-of-paper) color provides an actual availability of colored inks at the newspaper's printing press. Many of our leading apparel stores across the country, in all fifty states, make use of this color.

In tests of consumers noting an advertisement, percentages of 82 percent for R.O.P. and 90 percent for SpectaColor have been achieved. These are high scores indeed. Regular usage by stores, week in, week out, however, as may be expected, cut down such high scores. Nevertheless, color captures attention and interest and outranks most black-and-white advertisements of similar kind in the same newspaper.

Having set up its contract, then, with the local newspapers, the retail store can proceed to schedule its advertising in any way that matches its overall advertising plan. The normal patterns for retailing differ for food, for apparel, for furnishings. The calendar week in Fig. 10 below shows graphically how the majority of stores schedule their advertising for food, apparel, and home furnishings in the news sections of daily and Sunday papers.

	Sun.	Mon.	Tues.	Wed.	Th.	Fri.	Sat.
Food	—	L	L	M	H	M	—
Apparel	H	—	L	M	H	M	—
Home furnishings	H	—	—	L	H	L	—

H — heavy advertising day
M — moderate advertising day
L — light advertising day
— none or practically none

FIG. 10   TYPICAL PATTERNS OF RETAIL ADVERTISING IN NEWSPAPERS IN ONE WEEK

The Advertising Department in its immediate planning stipulates the size and shape of advertisement it plans to run, designating it by line and column. Thus, it may send in an "insert order" for an advertisement 300 x 2 (spoken of as "300 on 2"), meaning 300 agate lines from top to bottom and extending over two columns of the paper. Thus, this advertisement is a total of 600 lines, and is suitable for a standard newspaper page. An advertisement of the same total lines can be 200 x 3 (200 lines across three columns), 150 x 4 or 120 x 5. (See Fig. 11.) Of course, an advertisement may be any size and shape (with certain minimal restrictions laid down by the newspaper) that will fit into a given newspaper format.

There are two such formats: the *standard* and the *tabloid*. The advertising linage of a standard newspaper provides for 2400 lines on an eight-column page. The linage of a tabloid newspaper provides for 1000 lines on a five-column page. (Some tabloids use narrower columns and allow for six columns or 1200 lines of advertising space.)

There is still another consideration in buying newspaper space. The least expensive way (apart from the additional savings of large contracts) is R.O.P. This stands for "run-of-paper" and means

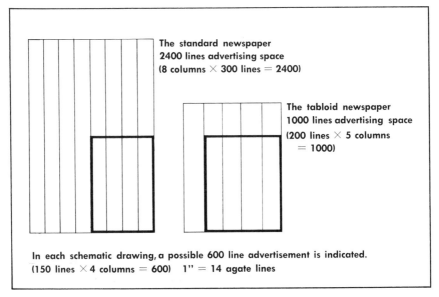

FIG. 11 NEWSPAPER LINAGE *(Approximate dimensions)*

that the newspaper production staff, in preparing the day's page layout of articles or editorial matter and advertisements, places the advertisements wherever they seem to fit best, and wherever they will enhance the make-up of the paper. This is not so dangerous as it sounds, since the newspaper is interested in good readership and will plan for an attractive newspaper. This means, in American journalism, placing the large space advertisements in the front section of the paper, but back of page 3. (In England, until a very few years ago, the prestigious *Times* of London placed advertising on its front (!) page.)

It is possible, however, to pay something extra per line and buy "preferred space" or "preferred position." This, often called "premium space," does indeed carry a premium price. But in this way a store can stipulate that its advertisement be placed on certain pages, such as the Women's Page (now more frequently called Food, Fashions, Furnishings), the Social Page, or the Sports Page, etc., or pages 2 through 5. It must always be remembered that good newspapers place certain restrictions on what can go on pages 1, 2, and 3 and what are the minimum dimensions it will accept for an advertisement.

Other favored positions are the back page of the entire newspaper, or the back page of an intermediate section. Large stores sometimes like to take seven columns in the standard-sized newspapers, permitting the 8th column to be used for news. In this way, it is thought by many that readership is increased for the advertisement.

The size of advertisements, the position in the newspaper, and the like, are often dictated by the tradition of the store, and in fact become an identifying mark of the advertising.

Magazines

Where retail stores use magazines for prestige, they most frequently use a full page. No other size will give them the impact and "presence" that they wanted when they initially included magazines in their plans.

When eventual sales of a product by personal visit or mail are the desired end-result of a retail advertisement, the store may use a page or a third of a page equivalent to one column.

For direct mail order, many, many stores use small advertisements, 1/6 of a page, or even less space, often measured by the column-inch.

Thus, magazine space may be bought by the page or fraction of a page, generally expressed in 1/3's and 1/6's, and, for small-space advertising, by the inch. Depending on the book (magazine), half pages and quarter pages may be used, too.

The series of sketches in Figs. 12a and 12b indicates the variety of size and shapes that can be bought in the magazine world.

A buy of a full page means a "non-bleed" page; *i.e.,* the advertising material is confined within the normal margins of that magazine.

A "bleed" page refers to an advertisement whose illustration or background extends right to the edges of the page, as the reader looks at it. Actually, it extends *beyond* these actual limits and is cut to size as the magazine pages are cut for binding. For this reason a bleed page is always more expensive to the advertiser.

FIG. 12   MAGAZINE SPACE

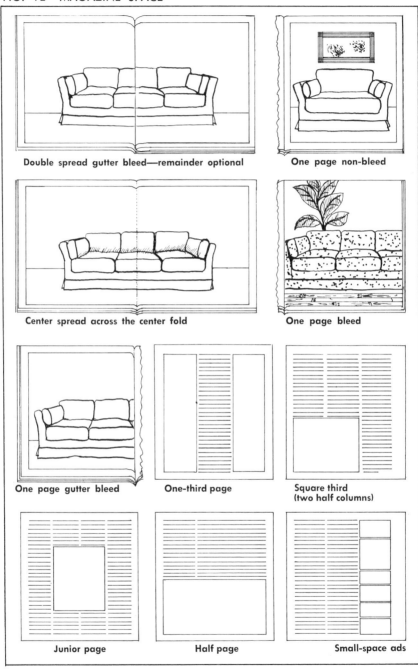

Double spread gutter bleed—remainder optional

One page non-bleed

Center spread across the center fold

One page bleed

One page gutter bleed

One-third page

Square third
(two half columns)

Junior page

Half page

Small-space ads

An advertisement can "bleed in the gutter"—that is, it can extend into the center binding of the book. This generally makes good sense only if the opposite page is planned as the second half of the advertisement, so that together they make what is called a "double spread."

A "center spread" is a two-page single advertisement run in one continuous spread across the center-fold of the book. (Note that the word "book" is a professional synonym for "magazine.")

Generally, as the reader has surely observed, magazines divide their pages vertically into three columns. This provides the possibility of buying 1/3 of a page where the column of reading matter is in the center. Two-thirds of a page, if sold, will generally require that the reading matter be placed toward the outside or the inside of the page. It is feasible to buy the two outside columns with reading matter between. There is also a "square third" available. This is actually two half-columns, or 2/6 of a page, making 1/3 of a page placed squarely on the page.

It must be kept in mind that any size advertisement less than a full page or 2/3 of a page will share a page with other advertising, just as is true of anything less than roughly a full page in a newspaper.

The "junior page" can best be described by explaining its origin. National advertisers who plan to advertise in various publications must, if they choose publications of varying sizes, prepare "mechanicals," or engraver's plates, for each size book. With the great size differential between, let us say, *Reader's Digest* and *Vogue*, they might be reluctant to include the larger magazine in their schedule if they have already planned production for the smaller size. The old *Saturday Evening Post* was among the first to offer a space in the middle of the page exactly the size of a *Reader's Digest* page, to make it worthwhile for an advertiser to spread his schedule into the larger magazine. It is true, of course, that he would be paying for the additional space, but he would not have to add anything at all to his costs of producing the advertisement. While usually still found in mid-page, the junior page can be seen in corners of the large magazines, from time to time. It is not in general usage by retailers, though it certainly could be.

In magazines, there is *no* premium position (cf. the newspaper discussion), except the inside of the front cover, the inside and outside of the back cover, and the center spread. The technical reference to the first three described is: 2nd cover, 3rd cover, 4th cover.

Other than these positions, the magazine's production department sets the advertisements in as these seem appropriate to the layout of the magazine as a whole. Sometimes, there are serious complaints among advertisers as one soft drink fights another across the page. However, retailers who use magazines are usually sophisticated about juxtaposition. Yet, they, too, fight for *front* position. Although studies are not conclusive on the subject, most advertisers persist in the view that the front pages of a magazine are more surely, and certainly more immediately, read than the back pages.

Costs of Print Media

What is the cost of print media? That is, what does the advertiser have to pay for his newspaper or magazine space? It would be impossible, and of little value, to try to list costs of newspapers and of magazines here.

There is, however, a publication issued monthly, *Standard Rate and Data Service*, which provides information on all quantitative facets of media. The information is issued in the form of separate large paper-bound books under these headings, which can be of interest to retail advertisers.

Newspapers
Consumer Magazines and Farm Publications
Networks (TV; Radio)
Spot TV
Spot Radio
Transit Advertising
Direct Mail Lists

Other books in the series are of less or no importance to the retail advertiser.

In the case of print media, among the kinds of information given in a listing in SRDS are: address, telephone number, type of publication, time and method of circulation, circulation figures, circulation patterns, costs of all types of space that the publication will accept, production information as to page size, column width, requirements for reproduction, closing dates, and so forth.

No general listing could or should be given here. Particularly is this true for newspaper rates, since, as has been stated repeatedly, local rates are *not* printed, but are arranged between the newspaper and the local retail store.

Nevertheless, certain fundamentals of the cost theory can and must be summarized here. In brief, media costs are *based on actual, audited circulation figures.*

"Circulation" corresponds roughly to the number of copies of a given publication printed and distributed. Costs have nothing to do with the size of the publication (magazine or newspaper), nor the elegance of the stock on which it is printed. To paraphrase Shakespeare, *Circulation is all!*

Thus, a widely circulated magazine like *Reader's Digest* costs far more per page (small as that page is) than an elegant, more select publication like *Town and Country.*

One might ask, "Does anyone set the rates?", or "How can an advertiser compare the value of two newspapers, or two magazines?"

To answer the first question, no one sets the rate. Each publication knows its own cost of printing and circulating, knows what it can charge the reader or subscriber per copy. Of course, the cost to the purchaser of a newspaper or a magazine, especially of a newspaper, is miniscule, so small in comparision to the cost of getting out the paper that the two almost may be said to have no relation at all. However, to return to the previous statement, knowing its own costs and income the publication must set its rates at a figure that it hopes will provide a reasonable profit margin. Certainly, the cost to the advertiser must be one that "the traffic will bear."

Thus, the very next question must be answered: "How can an advertiser compare costs?" Of course, the industry has an answer, because it, too, asks the question.

For newspapers, advertisers use the "Milline Rate." This is the cost of an agate line of advertising reaching one million readers.[1] This may be arrived at in the following formula:

$$\text{Milline Rate} = \frac{\text{Actual Line Rate} \times 1,000,000}{\text{Actual circulation}}$$

For example, if Newspaper "A" has a line rate of $2.10 and a circulation of 300,000 and Newspaper "B" is $3.50 with a circulation of 700,000, the value in reaching people can be calculated and compared this way:

$$\textit{Newspaper A}: \quad \frac{\$2.10 \times 1,000,000}{300,000} = \$7 \text{ (milline rate)}$$

$$\textit{Newspaper B}: \quad \frac{\$3.50 \times 1,000,000}{700,000} = \$5 \text{ (milline rate)}$$

Thus, the more expensive line rate is actually the more economical buy, on the sole basis of numbers—a quantitative analysis.

Our earlier discussion of the qualitative analyses of a store's real or potential customers should certainly make it clear that a store must consider more than just numbers and milline rate. A retailer must think hard about the characteristics both of the publication (whether newspaper or magazine) and of the readers in making a selection of media. Here, however, we are weighing circulation and costs only.

For magazines, there is a "similar but different" formula which provides the advertiser with a comparable quantitative comparison, this time based on "Cost per Thousand" (cpm or C/M). This equation informs the advertiser of the cost of reaching 1,000 readers with one black-and-white page of advertising.

$$\text{CPM} = \frac{\text{Cost of B/W page} \times 1,000}{\text{Actual circulation}}$$

To explain further, let us assume Magazine "A" has a circulation of 400,000 and a B/W page rate of $8,000, while Magazine "B" has a circulation of 1,500,000 and a B/W page rate of $22,500.

$$\textit{Magazine A}: \quad \frac{\$8,000 \times 1,000}{400,000} = \$20 \text{ CPM}$$

$$\textit{Magazine B}: \quad \frac{\$22,500 \times 1,000}{1,500,000} = \$15 \text{ CPM}$$

Obviously, if numbers are all that are to be compared, Magazine "B," despite its higher page cost, is the better buy.

Again, it should be stated that costs are never exactly proportionate to the circulation figures. Therefore, both the "Milline Rate" and the "Cost per Thousand" are extremely helpful.

Costs of Broadcast Media

Some of what has been said about the cost of print media may be repeated here about radio and television costs.

First, costs are based on numbers of listening audience. Second, comparative costs can be scanned by using the Cost-per-Thousand formula. Third, contracts provide increasing discounts for increasing use.

But for the rest, the differences are far greater than any similarities. However, what applies to radio generally applies to television as well.

To begin with, the buys are in terms of seconds of length, of hours of the day, of frequency during the day and during a given week, and of the number of weeks in the season, originally 13, now often a variation of that figure.

Next, the listening audience changes not so dramatically from station to station as it does from one period of the day to another. In fact, for radio, one of the regularly active research organizations (Pulse) can supply audience figures at 15-minute intervals, an indication of the sensitivity of that medium.

Weekday patterns differ strongly from weekend patterns of listening. Summer months show audience differences compared with the rest of the year.

These characteristics contribute to the difficulty of getting a cold mathematical figure for Cost per Thousand, which we saw above was a valid measurement for print media and which is given as a guide to broadcast media, too. Nonetheless, there is none of the precision of counting newspapers or magazines printed and sold; no sworn affidavit on figures as specific as those. Stations subscribe to—in fact support—independent research on listener-figures. These can be used on the basis of the cost of a minute of broadcasting to determine the CPM (Cost per Thousand).

An advertiser may buy "R.O.S.," a specific time slot, "prime time", or a "package." An advertiser may buy all minutes, all 30-seconds, or a combination of these, and add some 10-second spots or "I.D.'s" (identification spots).

"R.O.S." (run-of-station), the alert reader will guess, derives from R.O.P., and means much the same. It provides for an economical buy of a given schedule placed, at the station director's discretion, across the day's broadcasting.

If time slots are stipulated by the advertiser, they may be in "prime time," shown as Class "AA" or Class "AAA." The advertiser may choose any other time slot, from these triple or double A classes down to Class "C" and, in some station lists, Class "D."

On radio, prime time is driving time, 6 A.M. to 9 A.M. and 5 to 7 P.M., a reflection of the importance car radios have had on listenership. On television, prime time is 7 to 11 P.M. In both media, costs are naturally higher for Class "AAA" spots, and they diminish as the designation goes through the alphabet.

It must be remembered that the characteristics of the program and of the listener-audience must be considered. This is important where one station or one time slot is cheaper than another. But it must also be kept in mind in the reverse case. The most expensive time may not be the best time for your store's commercials. Perhaps an 11 A.M. spot may be best for reaching your customer. Perhaps you would be best advised to schedule your commercials in the hour or so after lunch, when the young mother puts the baby into his crib for a nap, and she herself (if she is wise) settles down for some relaxation with a second cup of coffee or tea. If off-hours are your time, rejoice! It becomes *your* store's prime time, then, at bargain prices.

Combinations of all kinds (time of day, day of week, length of commercial, etc.) are possible and should be explored.

In broadcasting, especially in radio, there is still another variable in the buying patterns, and that is buying a "personality." In this type of buy, the advertiser generally buys a 15-minute segment of a well-known personality, either a disc jockey (D.J.), an anchorman on a panel show, or a moderator in a talk show. This is equivalent to sponsorship of a small section of a big program. It is generally an expensive way to buy time.

Obviously, however, since we have already seen that higher media costs mean more people, we are buying listenership numbers here. Moreover, the personality brings an added and valuable feature to his ratings—loyalty on the part of his listeners. In other words, the audience not only listens, it buys what he recommends or appears to recommend.

On television, as large stores become accustomed to using the medium—and this is occurring all over the country—they may find it advantageous to sponsor an entire local broadcast of the news or the weather, or to share the sponsorship of a program.

Giant retail corporations like Sears are clearly in a position to use network (national) television. They do so in professionally skilled ways that carry their message nationwide. Sometimes there will be completely sponsored programs, other times brief commercials. But their television efforts are always directed to promoting the name of the store, to conveying the single message: This is a good place to shop.

FOOTNOTES

[1] Even if the newspaper does not have a circulation of one million readers, this method provides a basis of comparison if used for all pertinent newspapers alike.

13

DIRECT CONTACT MEDIA:
DIRECT MAIL;
TRANSIT MEDIA

The channels of communication already reviewed have been the expected, public media. But other ways to communicate with customers exist and are important to retailers. Some of the direct contact media are not necessarily those generally considered as "media" at all. But here is perhaps another justification for this particular book, to bring another point of view from which to scan the picture, and to add, if the author is lucky, a new idea or two.

Accordingly, in this chapter, under the new nomenclature, it is hoped that a good case can be made for including some new media: the store itself, electronic devices within the store; and the good, solid-foundation old one, direct mail. Transit advertising will be discussed here, as well, as a good possibility for retail stores, and an even better one to replace the presently disreputable outdoor signs. (Outdoor is, however, reviewed as well.)

The Store Itself

"Medium" signifies the *means* of conveying a message; in this case, a commercial message. Certainly, then, a retail store, in both its physical plant and in the atmosphere it generates, can—in fact, *must*—be termed a medium, and certainly the one that comes into the most direct contact with the customers.

As we begin to talk of the store itself as a medium, we automatically enter into areas already discussed, and placed outside the limits of pure advertising (see Chapter 5).

Windows, interior display, special events, are, in larger stores, the responsibility of departments other than advertising. Yet, treated *this way*, as part of the total communications mix, they contribute importantly to an image-creating contact with the customer. Moreover, in smaller stores, the actual work that goes into the planning and the carrying out of any functions connected with these activities is the responsibility of the person who handles the advertising.

But it is in a larger sense that one ought to view *the store as a medium*. What is the look of the store? What is the message that is given to the customer as she enters? What is the ambience (that favorite word of the 70's) that envelops the customer as she walks through the store, rides the escalators, stops at counters and racks?

Even the smell of the store, perhaps especially the smell, conveys a subtle impression. Mustiness? A fuddy-duddy store, old-fashioned, out-of-touch. Clean, sprightly air? A store that knows what it is doing, alert to the world. A light or a heady perfume (usually discreetly identified by a small card at doorway or elevator)? A fashion store, one that can provide leadership and authority for what is new and a little bit ahead.

A prominent New York store located on Fifth Avenue in New York City during 1971 instituted a "happiness" program to project a pleasant, smiling face to its customers. This was promoted through the salespeople who welcomed the customer with a smile, through the telephone operators who wished the caller a "Happy Day," through direct mail to the charge customers letting them in on the new plans for a continued program of welcome. Institutional advertising in the newspapers followed through to complete the happy note. In today's turmoil and confusion, shopping ought to be a happy experience, and a store should show a happy face.

In store-wide promotions, interior decorations express the very keynote that is carried outside of the store in newspaper advertis-

ing. Banners hanging from pillars, decorations on counter ledges
. . . the whole store should echo the basic idea.

In-Store Electronic Media

In the 70's, in-store electronic devices can be put to new uses. We
have been accustomed now to hearing the P.A. system (public-
address, loudspeaker systems) in highly promotional and discount
stores calling out special values. Sometimes it can become a game
for the customer.

"White sheets at Counter 27 are being reduced to $1 each for
one hour beginning now, 11 A.M. Rush to Counter 27!"

So far, this kind of promotion provides a lot of excitement for the
customer who happens to be in the store, happens to want white
sheets, and happens to hear the announcement. So far, it provides
fun, the pleasure of an unexpected bargain, a bonanza!

In this way, the P.A. system is the voice of the store, and can
announce anything appropriate to the customers who are already
in the store. Not only sale merchandise, but a fashion show; not
only a one-hour cut in price, but a special service can be carried
over the P.A. system. For example, stores sometimes complain
that their restaurant or snack-bar service is not profitable—too
busy at one given hour, and empty the rest of the time. Why not
use the P.A. system to announce steaming, hot coffee and Danish
in the quiet morning hours, or a refreshing cold drink and a sand-
wich to pick up the afternoon shopper? This is one of a million
uses that could extend the serviceability of this electronic medium.

In the 60's, closed-circuit television in retail stores had limited
use. Asked about it, one class of college students replied, without
exception, that closed-circuit TV was a device used to detect and
apprehend shoplifters. What a sad commentary!

Certainly in the 70's, there is greater and more imaginative use
to be made of this medium than to act as a silent detective, however necessary that duty may be. Certainly, in the 70's alert retailers can use closed-circuit television to show and tell and
demonstrate. It can carry fashion news or home furnishings news
to different parts of a large store.

What about the snack bars and restaurants in the stores? Why
force your patrons to read and re-read the menu for something to

do during the often long wait for seating, or for service, or during the meal itself.

Now all stores have or can plan to have live fashion shows. Why not have a fashion show taking place in one part of the store beamed to other floors, to the eating areas? Why not a videotape re-showing of a successful, closed fashion show? Why not a good demonstration, with a deft technician busily at work in house-wares, beamed to the store's snack bar, home-furnishings area, or anywhere it seems right?

This author has sat (deliberately not making waves) in the credit office of one of the largest stores in the country, holding a plastic number, and has waited for *one hour* for that number to be called while the little powers that be checked to see if her application deserved their magical gift of credit—with nothing to do, nothing to see. Aside from the stupidity of the whole procedure (your author's credit is A-1, rest easy!), what a waste of good air and space. Why couldn't a closed-circuit TV have been enticing the waiting prospective charge customer with all kinds of goods and services that this great store (great in spite of its poor policy in that office) had to offer? Maybe a view of all the branches would be appropriate right there in the main office. We are a mobile society and the fact that one picks up a charge-card in Brooklyn does not mean that one may not be shopping the very next week in Manhasset.[1]

Again, as in the case of the P.A. system, these few suggestions are not meant to limit but to indicate just the bare beginning of the wider use of a current medium of communication that bespeaks "today!"

Direct Advertising

If the P.A. system and closed-circuit television are comparatively new internal media, one medium under consideration is not new at all. Direct advertising—the passing out of handbills, of flyers, within the store is certainly as old as retailing itself.

It is still a valid means of communicating with the customers. It provides a new-as-today kind of advertising on the spot, in the store.

Its great advantages lie in this immediacy, this on-the-spot urgency, and its daily "new-ness." It provides, too, an inexpensive medium for items that may be limited in number, where a newspaper advertisement would not be justified. It has, too, a private quality, suggesting that "for you who are here *today*, this store has some really good buys."

Almost the only disadvantage lies not with the flyer but with most of the customers, who litter the floor with the papers after a quick glance. Housekeeping is always a problem. This simply adds to the need for constant attention. The provision (to the despair of the advertising copywriters) of adequate trash baskets ironically close to the very place where the flyers are made available would solve a part of the problem.

Direct Mail

Closely allied to direct advertising is, of course, another old friend among media: direct mail.

Direct mail, which can cover everything from a 100-page Christmas catalog to a postcard announcing a sale, must be part of every retailer's advertising program.

It will not occupy the same position of importance nor be used for the same purposes by every retail advertiser, but in its very flexibility lies its greatest asset.

A retailer can use direct mail at will, any time, and with any frequency or infrequency. He can reach out to all his present customers, or any part of them. He can separate his charge customers from his cash customers, his actual from his prospective customers. And for each method he uses, he can find sound advantages.

The *flexibility* of the medium is not to be matched. The advertiser is, of course, the sole decision-maker of what goes out, how many, to whom, and at what cost.

It has a *universality* of purpose. Every objective of advertising and promotion can be served by direct mail. It can sell actual products. It can invite customers (old, new, potential) to visit (or re-visit) the store. It can advise them of new merchandise, new departments, new policies. These are the most elementary of uses to which direct mail can be put.

Direct mail, while not an inexpensive medium at all, is yet highly "*accountable*." Take a mailing with a specific objective (to sell a certain product, to open up charge accounts, to get customers into a private sale, etc.), where the cost of the mailing is known. It is certainly simple to figure up your bills. Then the results can be measured against these costs to give a very precise return figure.

Thus, if a store plans a mailing to open up new charge accounts, it can follow the formula:

$$\frac{\text{Cost of each charge}}{\text{account opened}} = \frac{\text{Total cost of mailing \& postage}}{\text{No. actual accts. opened}}$$

Specific store-figures have been nationally and individually compiled to determine the value of charge customers. Results indicate that charge accounts help to increase the frequency as well as the dollar-value of purchases over those of non-charge customers. It is, therefore, very well worthwhile to a store to institute a regular program in at least three specific directions:

1. to open new accounts
2. to make the current account-holder feel wanted, privileged, even pampered
3. to invite holders of unused accounts to become once again active as customers of the store.

Therefore, a retailer should plan to spend a reasonable sum at yearly intervals, or possibly every two years, to review its charge accounts, to make a real drive to increase the number of active accounts, whether through gaining new accounts, or reviving old, inactive ones. The pay-off will last for years.

Although this is but one of the many places where direct mail is especially valuable for the retailer, it has been dealt with at some length to show how this medium can yield results for the retail store and how the store can figure out values.

Outdoor and Transit Media

There remain to be discussed outdoor and transit media. Outdoor media include 24-sheet posters, painted bulletins, and spectaculars. Posters are literally large sheets of paper, each square reproducing one section of an advertisement; when 24 are pasted up in order, they form the total sign.

Painted boards are messages painted (in large squared copies of a miniature held by the painter) on wooden or metal boards.

Spectaculars are the illuminated, action-filled signs that are usually seen in the center of the city. They are elaborate, complicated, with moving devices, flashing lights, and even, in one famous sign on Broadway at Times Square, New York, belching smoke. Some seem to pour water, or orange juice, and so on, as far as the imagination can stretch.

In essence, outdoor advertising provides space for a quick, single message. For the retail store, it may carry the store name and serves mainly as a reminder. Sometimes, used on cross-country roads, an outdoor sign may serve as a "directory" for strangers coming onto a town, saying, roughly. "You are approaching Smithtown. Visit Jones' at Main and Court Streets." (Of course, no sign in the 1970's would be as old-fashioned as that, but the message is the same.)

It advantage lies in the terse, quick message. Its disadvantage, if we are talking of real "outdoor," lies in its irritant quality. This may need further explanation, although some has already been given in an earlier chapter.

This medium represents a highly visible means of communication, with which all of our readers will be familiar. As a matter of history, it was the first type of advertising to come under strong criticism, and the first to be regulated. It has been, in fact, banned from the sides of highways in two of our 50 states. Other states have strong sign and bulletin regulations. Many of our municipallities, towns, and village restrict the use, size, and style of street and outdoor store signs.

The incoming tourist is not aware of your town's regulations of signs and bulletins. If, therefore, your municipality has loose or no regulations, your store may be criticized (perhaps unfairly in your judgment) for "polluting" the incoming roads and highways.

Perhaps your store should be ahead of the town and be more rigid in the type of sign or bulletins it permits itself—if any at all. Care should cover size, placement, copy, artwork.

Earlier in this book, in connection with the function of advertising, some statements were made as to the necessary role of advertising in the years to come. Here, too, is a place for a retailer to take a leader's stand ahead of his competition. Again, it is never good business to irritate prospective customers. The environment is the retailer's as much as his customers', and it is to the best interest of all to preserve and protect what we have.

To return to the outline established for media treatment, how does a store buy [2] outdoor advertising? All types are bought on a rental basis from various groups who themselves have rented the highway space, street, rooftop, or "building side" spaces on long, long-term contracts. These companies have cleared or cleaned the area, put up the necessary superstructure, lights, or whatever is called for.

Furthermore and most importantly, if the company is run in an ethical and modern way, it has conducted research into each site for the passing of cars or pedestrians, whichever is appropriate to the site. It is on the basis of the *traffic count* that the company charges a certain rental price.

A careful check, often by electronic device, is made of automobiles on a thoroughfare or highway coming toward and passing the sign-site. In case of city boards and signs, the check is made in either or both of two ways: of automobile traffic passing and of people walking past a given area on foot.

The advertiser can buy (rent) space for a brief period, but usually not for less than 90 days. Much longer periods are more customary.

Sometimes one site is included in the lease; often many sites. "Showings," the name given to the placement of advertising on an outdoor surface, are sometimes sold in groups. This would be particularly true, obviously, of posters. The reason is that posters (the sheets of paper pasted up) are reproduced by silk-screen in some multiple quantity of 100, 1,000, and so forth. It is clear that no one would rent one site to post one poster.

Bearing in mind, then, that "one poster" or "one sign" is an unreal, academic situation, however, just for the sake of our mathematics, a cost-per-thousand figure can be arrived at in the way with which our readers will be familiar by now:

$$CPM = \frac{\text{Actual rental of 1 Showing 1 month} \times 1,000}{\text{No. of persons (or autos) passing in 1 mo.}}$$

or more realistically:

$$CPM = \frac{\text{Actual rental of all showings bought 1 mo.} \times 1,000}{\text{No. of of persons (or cars) passing all showings in 1 mo.}}$$

Any unit of time (month, week, day, etc.) can be used, and even a total exposure for a full rental period. One must merely remember to use the same unit of time for the cost in the numerator as for the traffic count in the denominator, and to name the CPM appropriately—that is the cost per thousand will represent the cost of a month, a week, a day, or a year—whatever is used. It must be stated, however, that for purposes of finding comparative costs, these odd units of time would not be satisfactory. Unless needed for some specific, individual purpose, the basic rate for one month is most satisfactory.

Much the same arrangements, criticisms, and methods of buying and calculating apply to transit advertising. But first, let us explain the terms that are generally used in all discussions.

By transit advertising *posters* are meant: in subway and railroad stations and at airport terminals; and the *cards* used on the inside and outside of buses, on trains, subways as well as (where they are still running) on trolleys.

These "car cards" and posters are bought on two bases: by routes selected, and by total or fractional portion of buses, trains, or trolleys leaving a given terminal or garage. Again, underneath these two transactional methods, is the traffic factor. Certain routes provide greater passenger-carrying service, and on this rests the value for rental costs of space in the cars or buses of such lines. Certainly, buying a total run provides more of these passengers than in a fractional run. Again, this should be clear and needs no elaboration.

The companies that sell (lease) transit advertising space have sophisticated research and can provide full data and costs both on an individual and on a cost-per-thousand basis. (To obtain the latter figure for oneself, the same formula as that applied to outdoor advertising may be used here.)

The use of transit advertising by retail stores would vary from city to city, from suburb to surburb. Wherever a store considers that its patrons ride buses, subways, or other public conveyance to get from home to shopping, that store can wisely use transit advertising. Where this is not the case, if a store gains its patronage from its immediate neighborhood only, or only from those who drive their own cars, then transit advertising is a waste.

If used at all, the message should be short and quick to read. It should not be of an "immediate" nature, for no matter what stipulations are made in the contract for frequent changes, the store is at the mercy of another company's personnel.

Long after the card or poster should be removed, it still remains. As observers, we have all seen the Christmas poster in February. A store should care about this, should watch the service it receives, and register serious complaint if the change-factor is ignored.

In summary, then, of this and the preceding chapter, newspapers remain, as of this writing, the major public medium for retailers. Unquestionably, however, retailers have become accustomed users of radio. And, in the case of the giant chains and stores, the use of television is growing year by year.

FOOTNOTES

[1] Apologies to non-New Yorkers. These are respectively, a borough of New York, and a town on Long Island.

[2] "Buy" is used, as is customary, although "rent" would be more accurate.

PART FOUR

CREATING
THE ADVERTISING

The creation of advertising provides one of the most stimulating careers open to well-prepared young people. It is a career not easily handled by a narrow, "organization-mind" mentality. While providing excitement and challenge, it demands someone who will not "take off into space," but is soundly grounded in the concepts covered in preceding chapters.

Now we are ready to explore the writing, illustrating, and production of the advertising message.

One chapter in this section will cover the readiness of the copywriter to write. The next two will provide some aid in the writing of print and broadcast copy. A chapter will talk about the visual of the advertisement. Finally, a chapter will serve as a "wrap-up" of all the creative elements and activities for promotion within the whole store.

14

READY TO WRITE
THE ADVERTISEMENT?

Under the larger topic of creating the advertising, there must be included:

1. The written part of the advertisement
2. The visual part of the advertisement.

Copy is the word used to cover the written part of the message, *all* the written portion. This includes the headline, the body copy with its own structure and the important closing, the legal signature of the store or its logotype, and store information.

The *visual* part covers not only the very obvious illustration, whether photograph or sketch, but also the entire arrangement of the copy and artwork in relation to the space (white space) the advertisement will occupy. This visual relationship is called the *layout.*

No one, it is hoped, is so misguided as to enter into any controversy about the comparative importance of copy and artwork. The total pattern formed by the configuration of the words and artwork together carries the meaning and stamps the impression on the consumer's mind. Together, copy and artwork form the message the advertiser wants to convey.

The creation and preparation of an advertisement must start somewhere, and they generally start with the copy concept, and thus with the copywriter. This has been commented upon frequently throughout the book, principally in the early chapters on organization and functions.

It is time now to suppose that you are seated at a desk in the Advertising Department, with merchandise in front of you. Or it may be you are seated in a small corner of your retail store.

The large admonitions are over; the concepts have been digested. Now, with the merchandise surrounding your desk, is the "moment of truth." You have been assigned to write copy.

What "large admonitions?" What "concepts?" Now is the time to particularize those all-encompassing considerations. We may take a look backward over these pages, but it will be with a •different, very specific approach.

As you begin to write, you must think of the store you are working for, the product you have to write about, the kind of advertisement your copy will go into, the medium it will run in. Then overall, perhaps all of the time, you must keep thinking of the potential customer who reacts to all of these elements. A store uses a medium to put out a message about a product. Perhaps a rough diagram will help to clarify this (Fig. 13).

FIG. 13 INTERACTION OF PROMOTION AND THE CUSTOMER

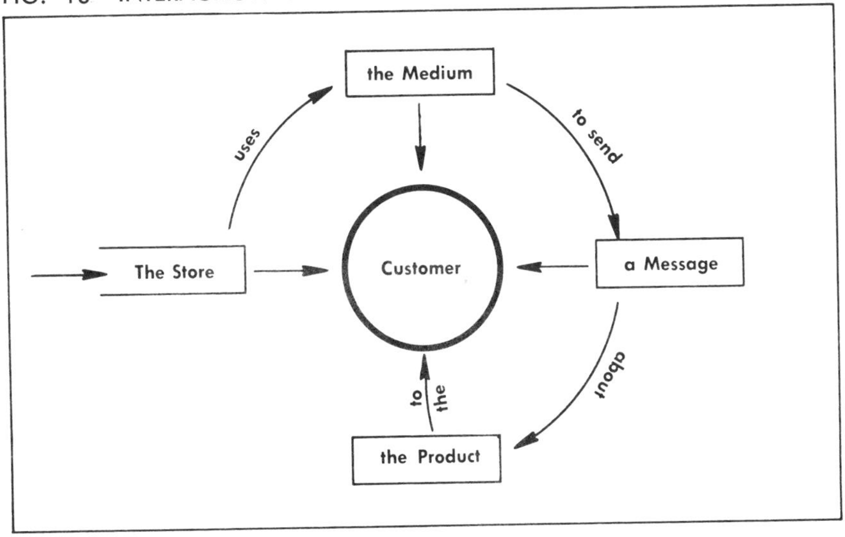

Store Factors

For what kind of store are you writing today? In an earlier chapter (Ch. 8), we discussed the interlocking possibilities of prestige stores handling their advertising in a "promotional" way. The copy you write must take cognizance of the store's own view of itself and of the way it wants its customers to view it. These two mingle in what may be termed "store policy."

Your job is to convey that policy to the readers of your advertising. Every piece of copy, no matter what its immediate subject, must reinforce the store as a whole.

That is possibly as important a job as copywriters can have. Where an error in this area is made, it may be observed that it is invariably the copy that oversells beyond the capabilities of the store to deliver. Too often, the copy conveys a sense of leadership, of friendliness, of fine quality and integrity that the store itself does not possess. The consumer (in such a case she rarely gets to be a "customer") reads the advertising and gains some impression of the store. Then she visits that store, only to have the equivalent of cold water thrown at her in the guise of surly employees, unattractive merchandise, poor "housekeeping," and a general air of seediness. The reverse, oddly enough, is rare, for a truly modern, well-run store will have an alert advertising department that knows how to deliver the appropriate message.

So, it does not pay to oversell the store. "Sell it like it is!"

Nevertheless, it must be borne in mind that a dynamic store moves forward whatever its size or type, and its policies move along some charted path. The policies are conveyed to the outside world through the store's image or reputation, and these change. It is the business of the copywriter to be aware of this movement. Thus copy written by the same copywriter over a length of time may have a different underlying core or theme, as the writer grows with the store.

Product Factors

Now, again, as we supposed earlier, you have the merchandise on your desk. What is it? Let us say it's a group of handbags. They

BUYER'S INFORMATION FOR ADVERTISING

(Must be accompanied by merchandise samples)

Important selling features

List in order of importance the selling features (and benefits to the consumer) that you consider the most important reason why the customer should buy this merchandise. Tell us why this merchandise is superior to similar offerings she may have seen.

Be specific. Do not attempt to write the copy, but indicate clearly, and in your own terms, the reasons why YOU bought this particular merchandise. Given this information, we will endeavor to translate it into an enthusiastic and persuasive advertisement aimed at convincing the customer that this is merchandise she needs, wants and should buy.

Please do NOT list price or savings here (use box at right).

(Main Feature)

1. _____
2. _____
3. _____
4. _____
5. _____
6. _____
7. _____
8. _____
9. _____
10. _____

(If necessary, use other side for additional information)

Have you included MATERIAL? FIBER CONTENT? WASHABILITY? SIZES? COLORS? NO IRON? FINISHES? FAMOUS BRANDS?

_____ _____
Buyer's signature   (Date)

Dept. No. _____
Day of week _____
Date _____
Paper _____
Linage _____

☐ This is a repeat ad.
See _____ (paper) _____ (date)
For copy _____ Art _____
General approach _____

☐ This offering should be keyed for selling starting on _____ (day of week)

☐ **REQUEST FOR NEW ARTWORK**
List number of illustrations required, indicating item to be featured, if any.
_____
_____
_____
Detailed information regarding artwork must be attached to merchandise samples. (Use Form 32643)

☐ There is a vendor allowance in connection with this advertisement in the amount of $ _____

PRICE
_____ each, _____ pair, _____ set

☐ I have requested a comparative price and I have sent copy of this form together with samples to the Comparison Office.
regularly _____ usually _____
formerly _____ originally _____
manufacturer's list price _____

MAIL AND PHONE SOLICITATION
☐ Mail and phone orders filled within 5 days of receipt of order.
☐ Mail and phone orders filled on _____ or more.
☐ Mail and phone orders filled while quantities last.
☐ No mail or phone orders

SHIPPING CHARGES
☐ Beyond motor delivery area add _____ $ for handling.
☐ For each additional unit add only _____ $ for handling.
☐ Beyond motor delivery area, express charges will be collected on delivery.
☐ Plus small charge for home delivery.

CREDIT
☐ THIS OFFERING WILL BE SOLD ON CREDIT ONLY $ _____ DOWN, _____ MONTHS TO PAY.

BRANCH PARTICIPATION
☐ ALSO AT _____ ☐ ☐ ALSO AT _____
☐ ALSO AT _____ ☐ ☐ _____ STORE ONLY

ILLUSTRATION 7   Buyer's Request for Advertising

should be accompanied by a "Request for Advertising," a form filled in by the buyer, telling the Advertising Department many of the features of the merchandise, price and construction, among other details. (See Ill. 7).

In addition to the merchandise details, the important features of the project, generally referred to as *selling points*, should be listed. Again, depending on the merchandise, it can include woods, finishes, performance, care, and the like. The product features or selling points of this line of handbags would be shown on the buyer's Information Sheet, information about shapes, colors, leathers, linings, and so on.

It must be remembered that the buyer treats the portion of money to be spent on the stock as a precious trust. Sometimes mistakes are made, but every good buyer chooses carefully so that, basically, the department is stocked with the merchandise he believes his store's customers will want. Of this stock, he can select only a small fraction to promote through advertising, display, or both.

It is, then, important for the buyer to get across to the Advertising Department the very specific reasons that Item A (not Item B) was selected for advertising. There must be reasons, and the copywriter must know them, through actual statement, or perceive them in some way in order to write effective copy.

In the best of all possible worlds, there is and should be good rapport between the copywriter and the buyer. They ought to try to understand each other. It is a cliché to say they both have the same goals at stake: *successfully and profitably to promote and sell the merchandise of the store.*

However it comes about, the copywriter, who must know all about the product, must also know how to translate the product features into product benefits for the consumer.

In *institutional* advertising, the above two factors, store and product, merge. The store *is* the product, the product *is* the store. Together they form the single core of the selling message. The store, just as a product, has characteristics or features that become selling points and finally are transmuted into *benefits* that can be provided to the consumer. (See Ill. 8.)

We're a wellspring of the freshest finds from all over the world.
We must be that way. Ours is a very special business . . . a concept people
count on. Bergdorf's has grown in its 71 years to become a cascade
of exclusive catches. We've our very own fur designer-in-residence,
Emeric Partos . . . our beautiful Bridal World of Monica Hickey . . . Lou Gartner's
special Needlepoint Place . . . the super snipsters in our unique Bigi Cutaway
. . . the high-stepping shoes in our Delman Salon . . . the Van Cleef & Arpels Boutique . . .
our Givenchy Nouvelle Boutique . . . Jean Louis Scherrer Shop . . . Tiktiner
Corner . . . and magnificent Mallets of London. They're all here. And all ours. To skim
the cream of fashion's crop, to corner prized collections, to bring in the best
is but half our job . . . to serve, to please is the rest.

*"Abundance" is the name of the lovely statue by Karl Bitter that's been gracing our front yard since 1915.

ON THE PLAZA • NEW YORK
**BERGDORF
GOODMAN**
5TH AVE., 57 TO 58TH STREETS

ILLUSTRATION 8   The Institutional Advertisement

Ad Factors

Given a review of what place the store occupies in the community, given the product and its selling points, we can move on to our next question.

What is this advertisement's objective? What is it supposed to accomplish for the store? What response is it hoped will be elicited from the consumer? Do you hope for actual sales tomorrow or in the coming week? Do you plan to create an awareness of the product, or of the department, or of the store?

These and other possibilities have already been discussed for an overall plan. Here, they are asked in a very narrow sense about one, two, or a half-dozen advertisements, the ones that need to be written today and tomorrow. You will have to answer these questions specifically before you write or complete the copy.

There are other "ad factors" that make a difference in the writing. Is this copy to be part of a whole series of advertisements your store is running? If so, it is said to be a part of a *campaign*. If it is, then you will be able to look back over other recent advertisements in the campaign to see what *unifying theme* runs through all of them. That is what makes them a campaign. You will then see how your current copy can be made to fit into the total picture.

Is it, on the other hand, a single advertisement to stand by itself with its own style and expected end-result?

Fandango colors. Red, green, yellow and violet kid sandal by Risque. 17.00. Matching handbag, 14.00. Young Colony® Shoes, sixth floor, Fifth Avenue, and branches.

ILLUSTRATION 9
A "Single Item" Advertisement

Is this copy, whether part of a campaign or not, part of a large, perhaps store-wide, promotion? Again, that promotion would have a pre-planned theme, and your copy must fit in.

These are going to make a real difference in your presentation of the selling message.

Finally, is the merchandise on your desk to be the subject of an advertisement by itself? In this case, if it is one product, your advertisement will be called "single item." (See Ill. 9.) If it is part of a group, as in the case of the handbags, where you stress the variety of styles and colors, it is called "assortment" advertising. (Ill. 10.) Against this type of unified product advertising, your store, particularly in its Sunday advertising, may choose to bring together a great variety of products from different departments on

ILLUSTRATION 10
Assortment Advertisements

one page in the newspaper. This kind of advertisement is called alternately "departmentalized" or a *"round-up."* (This author prefers the latter as more descriptive.) (Ill. 11.)

ILLUSTRATION 11   A "Round-up" Advertisement

Media Factors

It will help to write effectively if you know for what medium you are writing.

This sounds too elementary to bear much thought, especially after the full review in preceding chapters. Of course, there is a difference between television and the newspaper. But these broad definitions are not the only ones meant. It is helpful to know in which of two newspapers (if your town gives you the luxury of a choice) this particular advertisement is scheduled to run. Is it a morning newspaper? Is it an evening edition? The latter comes out on the stands in mid- or late afternoon. Is it a Sunday newspaper, regular news section or feature supplement?

In radio, as has already been said, different stations provide distinct personalities, both as a whole and program-by-program. It is important to know what kind of commercial "buy" your store has negotiated.

To return to print, there are other factors about the media buy for a particular advertisement that will somewhat affect the copy. What is the size of this advertisement? What shape has the Art Department stipulated for the total linage? In Chapter 12, diagrams indicated how linage in a newspaper was bought. The diagram on page 129 will indicate how an art director can lay out a 600-line advertisement, thus changing its shape. Your job as copywriter is to understand how to write for any suggested arrangement of lines and columns (Fig. 14).

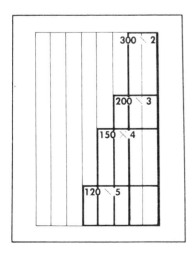

FIG. 14 VARIATIONS ON A 600-LINE SPACE

Sometimes, too, it helps to know whether special placement has been ordered. Surely, copy for a set of luggage would be handled one way if the space were to be in the Fashion and Foods Section (formerly called Women's Page), and in another way if it is to be placed in the Sports Section.

Finally, for the purposes of this discussion, a big question: Does your store plan to use color if it is offered by a newspaper in your city?

For fashion apparel, for men's haberdashery, for foods and cosmetics, what a great difference color can make in impact! And surely, your copy cannot help but be affected by your store's use of color.

To spell out the reverse, obvious though it may be, the use of "basic black-and-white," which is overwhelmingly the custom, demands of the copywriter commanding headlines at any time, but above all, a full and vivid vocabulary of color and strong, descriptive terms.

A third consideration is the deliberate dismissal of color in a newspaper that offers color. Probably such a newspaper has a good deal of retail advertising that is in color. If the merchandise lends itself to color, then the copywriter whose store's policy does not permit of this extra-dollar media buy certainly starts with a handicap for his message that is no less real because it *is* a store-made decision.

Customer Factors

Elsewhere in this text, and specifically in chapters 3 and 8, will be found a reasonably full discussion of the consumer and how he proceeds to make a purchase. At the point of writing the copy, it is again appropriate to think hard about *the consumer*, but this time, we may begin to call him *"the customer."* At this juncture, too, the thinking must be specific and precise.

"Who is your store's logical customer?" is a question that has been asked much earlier. Now the question is, "Who is the customer for the department, the line, *the very item*, that is in front of you?" Your earlier considerations in this area will stand you in good stead now.

Now you have only to take it down a step further, to think

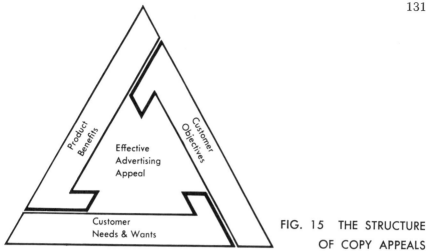

FIG. 15   THE STRUCTURE
OF COPY APPEALS

through to who are the possible purchasers of this item, this set of terrace furniture, this lawnmower, this long-skirted beachdress.

It is on the basis of your intelligent understanding of your customers and the product you are offering that you can begin to think about *copy appeal.* You must keep firmly in mind the outer and inner goals of your logical, potential customer. He has needs of which he is aware and which he can put into words, and, in addition, he has many unverbalized needs and wants.

What appeals can you bring the potential customer in your copy about a given product, that can promise both tangible and intangible satisfaction when the purchase is made?

This schematic drawing of copy structure may help the young writer to build toward effective appeals and, consequently, effective advertising. (See Fig. 15.)

(So far we have addressed ourselves strongly to the copywriter, but at least a hint can be thrown out that the artist, too, must provide this kind of support in the layout and the illustration so that the *whole* advertisement, the total configuration, can do its job.)

Specifically, then, if the copywriter has to write an advertisement for new Spring handbags, many appeals are open to him. First, he must look at the product or products: the merchandise. Some of the selling points and product benefits that could occur in this category of goods might include: low price or high price within reason, durability, versatility, finish, linings, fabrics (leather or non-leathers), a look of elegance, a variety of styles, colors, the fact (or not) of their being imported or produced by a well-known designer name.

It will be a rare handbag, indeed, that could be equally appealing on all of these counts. The product asortment you have been given to advertise will, in itself, eliminate some selling points, include others, and point the way to stressing still others.

For example, if the handbags represent a moderate- to high-priced special purchase, a collection at $29, no mail or phone orders accepted, you can eliminate the low-cost factor at once. Durability, or good-wearing qualities, variety of styles, fine leathers, smart colors, sizes; leather linings may not be a part of the collection. Imported? No, not this time, but they are by a well-known handbag designer-producer.

Next, consider your customer. Let us say you are employed by a specialty (not a department) store. Your customer, you have decided, is the career girl or suburban housewife with a reasonably good discretionary income, aware of the "right" fashion look, and ready at this time to buy parts of her Spring wardrobe. Fortunately this is the very customer who will be interested in these handbags. ("Fortunately" means you have a good buyer who knows her business, her customers, and her store.)

Now try to fathom your typical customer's *own* objective. (Yours is easy: to bring the customer into the store to buy some of these handbags.) What does she want to achieve through her purchase of a handbag? To get something to hold her wallet, glasses or sunglasses, some make-up, keys, maybe cigarettes, pencil and memo pad? Possibly all of this. To complete a new smart Spring wardrobe? Very likely. Then, maybe she needs more than one. But what else is her goal in reading your advertisement about handbags? She probably wants something for all the reasons we mentioned, and, in addition, she wants to feel secure and comfortably herself. She wants that accessory to make her feel good about all the other money she has spent, perhaps on a suit or a coat, or a few dresses, shoes certainly . . . and maybe this year, a new hat.

She may want one bag for the whole Spring, you say . . . and yet you can ask, is that really *our* store's typical customer?

Underneath it all, does she want a safe, albeit smart, handbag? Or, does she want the fun of picking and choosing, based upon her *conviction*, which your copy must have given her, that the values are right, the bags are smart, the quality good, the prices reasonable? Doesn't your customer want something extra in her bag or bags—a *panache*, a flair to finish her whole Spring fashion-look?

Of course, we've made the example fun to read about . . . a gay, with-it career girl, instead of a matron with four children. But in actual day-to-day writing, the copywriter gets a different kind of "fun," that of matching wits and ingenuity by writing to meet the customer's unverbalized, sometimes even unfelt, needs and objectives in deciding to buy.

If you analyze your product, your customer and *her* objectives soundly, your appeals will be on target.

This is not, in reality, a slow, long process through which the copywriter goes. In fact, the longer you are on the job, and the more successful you are, the faster the whole process becomes . . . until it is perhaps almost intuitive. Nevertheless, the wise and alert copywriter will check himself at intervals, just to be sure that he is on the right track, that he has kept abreast of his store, its policies, and the typical customer it attracts. So, once in a while, he will put himself through the whole process again.

15

ELEMENTS OF PRINT COPY

Up to this point you have done little writing, and what there has been was of the "listing" and "jotting" type. You have, however, thought a great deal. You have used your grey matter to study and analyze all the factors described in the last chapter. You ought now know *why* you are about to write a piece of copy.

How will you put your ideas across to bridge that gap that lies between you and the customer? *What* words will you use? *Where* will you place them in the total copy structure? These are the considerations of this chapter.

Let us start by enumerating the ingredients of the "total copy structure." These include headline, subheadline (if one is used), the body copy, the closing, store signature, and store information. The latter refers to branch addresses, phone numbers, store hours, and the like. Into this total structure must go all the information and the appeal you have decided your copy will provide.

Copy Approach

How do you convey these ideas? There are three general ways you can write your copy. These are called copy "approaches."

First, there is the *factual approach*, which is a direct, logical presentation of your ideas about the product, its benefits, and appeal. This is the approach most frequently used in retail advertising. It allows for full descriptions, inclusion of unique details, and a maximum of information about construction and performance. All of these contribute to the writing of effective retail copy. An example of the factual approach is shown in Ill. 12.

Second, at the opposite end of the spectrum is the *narrative approach*. This is the writing style in which the copywriter cloaks the selling message and the product facts in a story-like sequence. The facts themselves may be given in a descriptive way, or a frankly fictitious situation may be set up. Furniture might carry copy that told of the "house that bought this sofa;" garden equipment could

ILLUSTRATION 12   Factual Approach

Sand dune silk

Silk pongee reappears, looking fresh in a cool and leisurely weekend suit. Precisely tailored, every detail scored and underscored in double rows of white stitching. It's all the color of windswept sand, in sizes small to extra large, $100. Country Gentlemen's Shop, Sixth Floor.

THE MEN'S STORE
SAKS FIFTH AVENUE
On mail and phone orders, please add sales tax where necessary. Beyond our regular delivery area, also include 75¢ handling charge. Sorry, no c o d's. New York • White Plains • Springfield • Garden City • Washington Bala Cynwyd • Boston • Atlanta • Chicago • Skokie • Detroit • Troy • St. Louis Palm Springs • Beverly Hills • Palo Alto • Phoenix • Miami Beach • Palm Beach • Ft. Lauderdale

be advertised as "the little mower that could." While this approach tells a story, it still has the task of presenting product information. It is pertinent to note, however, that retail advertising does not make heavy use of this approach. The best examples are to be found in national advertising. A good narrative example in retailing is cited in Ill. 13; a national example is shown in Ill. 14.

Between these two extremes lies the *emotional approach.* This

ILLUSTRATION 13
Narrative Approach

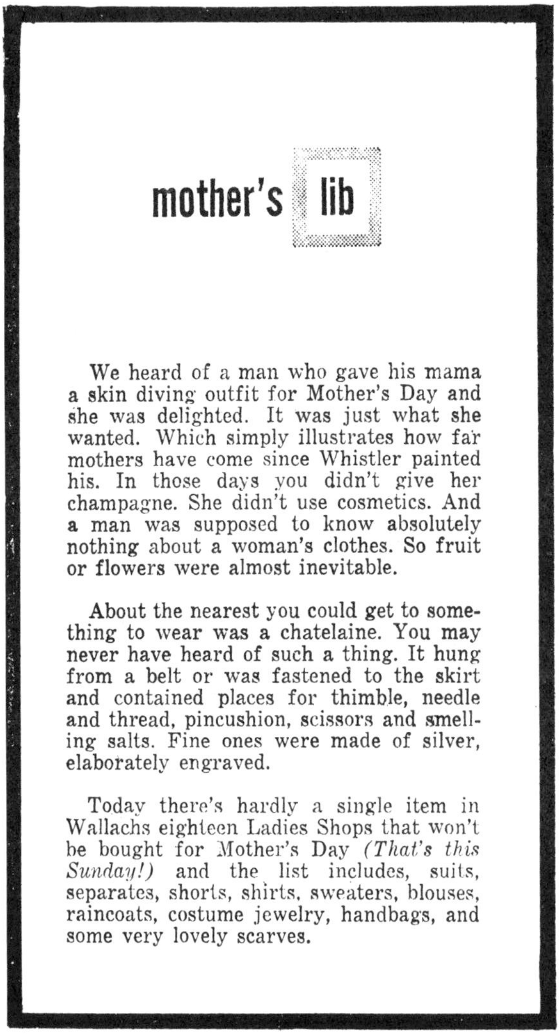

mother's lib

We heard of a man who gave his mama a skin diving outfit for Mother's Day and she was delighted. It was just what she wanted. Which simply illustrates how far mothers have come since Whistler painted his. In those days you didn't give her champagne. She didn't use cosmetics. And a man was supposed to know absolutely nothing about a woman's clothes. So fruit or flowers were almost inevitable.

About the nearest you could get to something to wear was a chatelaine. You may never have heard of such a thing. It hung from a belt or was fastened to the skirt and contained places for thimble, needle and thread, pincushion, scissors and smelling salts. Fine ones were made of silver, elaborately engraved.

Today there's hardly a single item in Wallachs eighteen Ladies Shops that won't be bought for Mother's Day *(That's this Sunday!)* and the list includes, suits, separates, shorts, shirts, sweaters, blouses, raincoats, costume jewelry, handbags, and some very lovely scarves.

Thoughts expressed by above Moppets: (1) "There's nothing we can't solve together." (2) "I miss you." (3) "Our love is growing all the time." (4) "I thought about you and it made my whole day." (5) "Everybody needs a little security." (6) "I love you." Moppets © 1972 Fran Mar.

Moppets.

A collection of very special little people to make someone smile.

Wherever Moppets go, they spread happy thoughts of friendship, warmth and affection. To charm and captivate the hearts of all. Their innocent expressions and irresistible appeal are captured in hand-painted porcelain by Gorham. Couples $12, individuals $7.

From the Gift World of Gorham.
Gorham Division of Textron, Providence, R. I. © 1972 Gorham

ILLUSTRATION 14   Narrative Approach: National, not Retail Advertising

method of writing takes the facts and presents them in emotion-charged words, like "fiery," "floating," "earth-bound," and the like. Underneath the vocabulary, the advertising copy may be quite direct. This approach is widely used in retail advertising. (See Ill.

15.) In copy for fashion merchandise, apparel, shoes, cosmetics and similar products, it will be used very frequently.

The decision to use one approach or another depends on many elements, some already discussed, and some not specifically covered. The product, the price, the particular appeal to be used, the store's policy, and finally, the copywriter's own turn of mind, all contribute to the decision to use one rather than another of the possible approaches.

ILLUSTRATION 15   Emotional Approach

jean muir's new dresses speak
english/ body english/ jersies
and wools and crepe de chines
that float/ and flick/ and flow/
and flutter/ all now in the muir
shop on 2/ from $235/ come on
in/ and let them talk to you/

Henri Bendel

In each of the major approaches just outlined, there are the possibilities of a humorous or a poetic (actual verse) approach. These should be "handled with care." The reason may be obvious, but should be repeated here. Of all the kinds of writing *in any field,* the writing of poetry and of humor is probably the hardest. This may be because they demand sensitivity of a kind different from our normal, *prosaic* life. We speak and write *prose,* not poetry, in normal communications. As for humor, one man's sense of what is funny may leave another man glum, while moving another to hysteria.

Nevertheless, despite these cautions, if *you* can and if your product and store policy open up the possibility, you may find yourself writing some advertising that may be either poetry or humor. Of course, either of these sub-approaches can fall under any of the major ones: factual, narrative, or emotional. A light, pleasant touch of humor handles the selling message for the shoes in the example given (Ill. 16).

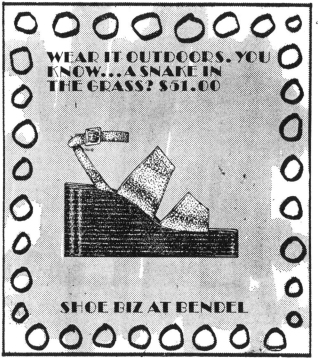

ILLUSTRATION 16
"Humor"

Another important sub-approach is that of *testimony or endorsement.* This can be factual or fictional (under the narrative approach). While this is a strong way of conveying selling ideas in national or trade advertising—and can or should be as strong for the retail level—it is not found too often in retail advertising. There is no real reason for this, except that it calls for careful, well-documented handling when used *factually.* A good case can be made against a retail store using *fictitious* testimony (except in obvious, good-natured humor). The retail store is too close to its customers, or should be. Its customers ought to be able to check with the store and ask, "Did she really say that?"

While apparel and furniture stores do not often use this approach, one kind of retailer does, in some few instances. That type of store is the supermarket. A few very successful chains have used real customers in their advertising to speak for the store, to point out certain products and to explain the services.

It is an excellent approach and, in examples that come to the mind of this writer, very successful. (It is too bad that they do not equally easily come to *hand,* to include here as examples. They are rare, and no current examples could be found.)

There is an offshoot of this approach, again more often used by the supermarket chains than by department stores. Sometimes, shopping centers use this device. This is the use of the "spokesman," a real person, either prominent or just "one of us," who is selected as a typical customer. The picture of this ideal shopper is used in such advertising, and some portion of the copy will be in his or her own words. This generally points out especially good buys or excellent services available.

The use of the "spokesman" sub-approach to underscore factual copy is a very strong tool. Especially today, when consumerism must become more than a hollow sound, this would be one way of talking to the consumer in her own language and of telling her some of the things she really wants to know about your store, your products, and your services. It would force the copywriter (and through him the store itself) to think in terms of and to "talk" to an actual customer-consumer, rather than to talk at her.

It goes without say that "Honesty in advertising" must be another phrase that is not hollowly echoed but really meant and acted upon. Through "spokesman" advertising, you might have a built-in control to be sure that your store means what it says. The person chosen, an actual member of the community, should be someone of standing and integrity who will not let himself be quoted except in solid, honest terms about honest product and service benefits.

Before dismissing fictitious testimony out of hand, it should be explained that this is sometimes described as monologue or dialogue, naturally depending on whether the fictitious experience is being told by one person, or related in a conversation between two people. This is, indeed, a useful device for radio or television commercials, and carries with it no stigma of "trying to deceive" in these media. In print, as has been suggested, it rarely comes off believably.

Finally, there is the old *"hard-sell"-"soft-sell"* controversy. Hard-sell is the term usually applied to heavy, strident sales advertising

ILLUSTRATION 17   Hard Sell: Ineffective Buckeye

ILLUSTRATION 19
Effective Hard Sell Copy

ILLUSTRATION 20   Effective Soft Sell Sale Copy

or to copy with extreme unprovable claims. Soft-sell, on the other hand, is copy with a light touch, in which the reader or listener is given good reasons to buy.

Frequently, although we are not covering artwork or layout in this chapter, the visual of the advertisement is a clear indicator of where the copy falls in this dual breakdown. Too often, the heavy inking and small type make the whole advertisement almost illegible (Ill. 17).

To help this, the copy facts are sometimes set out, not in complete sentences, but in what is called "bullet copy." This means single lines of product information each preceded by a heavy dot (therefore, the bullet) like this •. Sometimes these are squares, or other eye-catching single symbols. (See Ill. 18).

In the hard-sell advertisement, the language is that of the old cough-syrup-elixir variety. The whole feeling is one of trying to pull the customer into the store, push him into a corner, and make him buy.

Yet, not all sale copy, even that of hard-sell, need be that displeasing. There can be good reason for strong, even hard-selling copy. If everything comes together at the right time: product, place, price, opportunity, good writer, good art director, mixing everything in the right proportion, then hard-sell becomes what it should be: strong, effective advertising (Ill. 19).

Soft-sell advertising has all the better of it. It is, after all, *the style of today*. Whether product benefits are clearly stated or understated, the hoped-for feeling is one of "Let us sit down and reason together." The visual attempts to bring in tones of black rather than the heavy black in typography and art work. Layout can provide lots of white space to heighten the clean effect. The language of the copy pays some tribute to the consumer's intelligence and provides rational motivation.

Even a sales advertisement can be strongly effective with this more tasteful, soft-sell handling (Ill. 20).

The Headline

Everyone will tell you easily enough that it is the headline (with the artwork) that stops the eye and catches the attention. But, does every headline do this? Do they all do it equally well? Of course

Washington's Birthday Clearances and Specials

in our whole colony of 57 FS Stores scattered throughout the United States of America!

The Only Thing Fake:
Fake Fur Coats Of Templierra° Pile!
44.00
formerly 55.00
These are terrific Templierra° pile—a Borg° fabric—
all with fake fur trim. Knee lengths and pants coats, deep
and plush in Misses' sizes, on 2.
*Trademark of Borg° Textiles, a division of Bunker-Ramo Corp.

Equality For All!
Fantastic Dress Clearaway!
9.99 to 19.99
formerly 20.00 to 48.00
Grab every cent you can get your hands on!
Every important silhouette, color and fabric you can think
of. Misses', Jr., Jr. Petites. On 2 and 4.

Beautiful Boot-Top Skirts
9.99
formerly 15.00
These are the right skirts (just to the
boot-top) in all the right colors and
certainly the right savings. 5 to 15. On 4.

Come Across!
Super Pants Dress Special
23.99
These are new Spring pants dresses in all
sorts of silhouettes—smocks, shirts, tunics,
solids, contrast trims, contrast stitched,
white collar and cuffs. Great colors:
light, bright, dark. 8 to 18. On 2.

Great Knit Tops
6.99
formerly 12.00 to 16.00
Here are super savings on nylon and
Dacron° polyester knit tops—
all full fashioned, in many styles, great
colors. Get a bootload! 34 to 40. On 3.

WINTER WOOL COATS, formerly 65.00 to 75.00 . . . . .49.99

Grand Accessory Savings!

COSTUME JEWELRY, formerly 4.00 to 15.00 . . . . .1.99 to 7.49
BELTS, formerly 5.00 to 10.00 . . . . .2.99 to 3.99
HANDBAGS, formerly 14.00 to 27.00 . . . . .7.99 to 14.99

For The First Lady! Save On Intimate Apparel

LONG QUILTS, formerly 17.00 . . . . .8.99
HOSTESS LOUNGEWEAR, formerly 19.00 to 30.00 . . . . .10.99 to 18.99
BODY SUITS AND SKIRTS, formerly 6.00 and 7.00 . . . . .3.99
GOWNS, formerly 4.00 to 7.00 . . . . .2.99 and 3.99
½ OFF FAMOUS MAKER SHEER PANTYHOSE, formerly 3.00 . . . . .1.50
STRETCH BODY SUITS, RIB TURTLENECKS, formerly 9.00 . . . . .5.99

Big Savings For The Little Ones

GIRLS' RIBBED BODY SUITS, 7 to 14 . . . . .3.59
GIRLS' DENIM SLACKS, 7 to 14 . . . . .3.79

Be Nice To George!

MEN'S TWO PIECE CASUAL SUITS, formerly 45.00 . . . . .9.99
ITALIAN HAND MADE SILK TIES, formerly 7.50 to 10.00 . . . . .4.99

And In Our New York Store Only, Magnificent Mink Values!

FULL LENGTH NATURAL MINK COATS 599.00
NATURAL MINK STOLES 199.00
MINK AND LEATHER COATS, formerly 535.00 . . . . .399.00
JK ATELIER CONTEMPORARY FURS . . . . .20% to 40% off

More Coat Savings!

SUEDE COATS, formerly 100.00 to 150.00 . . . . .69.99 to 99.99
FUR TRIMMED COATS, formerly 140.00 to 200.00 .99.99 and 119.99
UNTRIMMED COATS, formerly 120.00 to 130.00 . . . . .69.99
THREE PIECE WOOL PANTS SUITS, formerly 80.00 to 90.00 . . . . .49.99

franklin
simon
FS

ILLUSTRATION 20   Effective Soft Sell Sale Copy

not. Then, what makes an eye-stopping headline? What else should it do? How do you write a good headline?

These are important questions, all calling for a reply. But first, let's throw in another question and answer that right now. Do you really write the headline first just because it generally comes first?

The simplest answer is, "No, not necessarily." One could add, "It's entirely up to the copywriter, to his own way of attacking a problem. The headline is like a title of a book. The contents of the book dictate what the headline should be." There is one difference, however, and that is a commanding difference. No one writes ten to fifteen books a day, and a copywriter often writes that number and more advertisements per day. So, the copywriter can easily have the whole advertisement in his head, so to speak, before he starts to write. Thus writing the headline *first* is often the simplest way to start. But not, by far, the only way.

The headline has many functions. First, we have already stated, is its eye-stopping function. Second, after that moment of gaining attention, an effective headline should roughly select the potentially interested audience. Something in those few words should say, "Go ahead, read on, this may very well interest you." Third, the good headline makes this selected person read on into the body copy to find out more. It ought not attempt to tell the whole story in itself. Fourth, a good headline should center around the major selling point of product benefit. An alternative to stating a selling point is to carry something of the copy appeal. This appeal is based one-third on selling points or benefits anyway. (See Fig. 15, page 131.)

The question of a sub-head is not worth too much concern. It follows naturally from the last-mentioned function. If the product benefit that needs to be given in the headline is two-fold (*e.g.*, convenience at low price), then a sub-head is called for.

Headlines are often classified by types.[1] It is difficult to avoid doing so for it helps the young copywriter to be able to choose among several kinds.

Since a good headline informs, selects, provides a hint of a benefit, and arouses curiosity, it follows that these four functions would make good classifications. Thus, each headline could be classified by a name, depending upon which of the four necessary functions the particular headline stressed; or, in the mind of the copywriter, which it *needed* to stress most strongly.

Briefly, then, the following are logically developed classifications, each of which may have some variation:

1. Informative headlines
   a. giving a product category
   b. giving real product news
   c. giving brand or store name
   d. announcing a store event
2. Curiosity-arousing
   a. through asking a question
   b. through a "gimmick" idea
   c. through a play on words
3. Providing a benefit
   a. by making a claim about the product
   b. by giving advice
   c. by making a promise
   d. by setting a mood (to meet hidden needs)
4. Selecting a potential customer
   a. by picking out one category, as, "Commuters!" (in a watch advertisement)
   b. by appearing to discard a group, as, "If you already own a Cadillac, turn the page!"

It is not necessary for a copywriter consciously to select a type of headline for an advertisement from a list and then to write "to type." It is far more important to remember that a headline is like a beckoning finger or Pied Piper, to catch attention and then lead the reader down into the body copy.

Retail headlines, in particular, must perform these services, unquestionably, by exciting, provocative words that promise some unique, special benefit. In retailing, the store does not too often use its own name in a headline. It is, therefore, more essential than ever that the headline point to the body copy as important to be read.

Body Copy and Closings

The heart of the advertisement is the body copy. It is the body copy that carries the selling message through which the store tells its potential customers about the products it offers, their benefits and advantages.

We have talked of the possible copy *approaches* (Ch. 14) that can be used, and we are now ready to talk about copy structure. Is there a logical way to present your ideas in a small piece of copy? Unquestionably, it is possible to organize advertising copy so that the customer receives a clear, cogent sales presentation. It is no more than one would expect from a good salesman.

First, whether you have written a headline or just thought about it, you must mentally have selected a *headline idea*—and that is where you start. Your body copy, however it proceeds, opens by saying something about the headline idea. It can expand upon that idea, underscore it, question it, repeat it, restate it another way. Any one of these is fine, so long as the body copy does open that way. That is the first step.

Now, we must take a second step, but here we had better remember we have three ways to go, three approaches: factual, narrative, or emotional. The last is a matter more of vocabulary and of "slant" than of any really different development; so it can fit into either of the first two plans. Let us take one road at a time.

The structure for the *factual approach* opens, as has been said, on a restatement of the headline idea. Retail body copy, which can be long or short, proceeds to give full details explaining the benefits hinted at in the headline idea. It then provides evidence to back up any claim or promise made.

Retail copy, particularly that for *volume* merchandise, can assist the reader in making up his mind in a variety of ways: by explaining how to use the merchandise or products; in the case of apparel, where to wear it, how to care for it, and so on. Here is the logical place to give the potential customer sound reasons to buy.

While copy space may seem limited, it is still necessary to keep this in mind: Tests have proved that, in staple and volume goods, the more product details given in an advertisement, the better the pulling power. That means that such copy is more effective in either creating traffic or inquiries in actual sales (always depending, of course, upon the original objective of the advertisement).

In retail body copy for prestige or high-fashion apparel, the headline idea must carry the fashion appeal, and the copy can then sketch in basic merchandising details to help the customer visualize the item. "Nuts and bolts" of construction, wearability, washability and so on generally do *not* add to the effectiveness of prestige advertising. On the other hand, explicitly spelled-out details of prestige service and special courtesies offered by such a store *do* create an effective advertisement that will often be talked about. When the customer mentions or actually uses the service features of the store featured in such an advertisement, the store is assured of that kind of copy's effectiveness.

In either case, if details have been either briefly sketched or thoroughly discussed in the copy, with evidence or proof of statements and claims that may have been made, then the body copy should come to a close.

Roughly two types of closing are possible. First, there is the *command* to the customer to take real action: telephone, write and mail, come in, try on, see for yourself, and the like. Second, the copy can close with a *soft suggestion*, where the hoped-for action is hinted at. For example, copy can close with a statement, "From now until Thursday." Translated, this means, "Better get in here before Thursday." A statement like, "Wouldn't you like to have one of your own?," really means: "Buy one."

A third possibility is no closing at all, or none that can be called a closing (for certainly the copy comes to an end). Almost without exception, this results in weak copy no matter how startling a beginning has been made. No good salesman leaves a customer without making an attempt to clinch the sale. No copywriter should consider his job done without giving the customer an opportunity to take real action. This has nothing to do with hard or soft sell. It is good common sense.

One of New York's most prestigious, limited-fashion specialty shops uses almost a slang approach to its command closings. It has established rapport with its customers both in its merchandising and in its advertising. It can say "Get down here fast!" It does not hesitate to do so, even for exclusive, one-of-a-kind two-hundred-dollar hostess gowns.

In the *narrative approach*, while the headline idea must be equally reemphasized at the start of the body copy, a looser form of development is possible.

The body copy starts by setting the stage for the product. After all, in narrative copy, whether you tell a story or develop a monologue or a conversation, the product is the star-maker of the little drama and, by extension, at the close, the potential customer becomes the star.

So, our copy development goes as follows: a restatement of the headline idea, the setting of the stage for the merchandise, bringing the item onstage, dramatizing it with description and details, then dropping the curtain in the closing with a clear direction to the customer: "Shouldn't you be a star, too?" or "Shouldn't you own this product to be a star?" In sum, the involvement of the potential customer with the product is made dramatically.

The closing, therefore, can be clearly stated or softly suggested, just as in the *factual approach.*

In any of the three approaches, merchandise details, such as sizes, colors, prices, and the like, are usually placed near or at the very end of the body copy. Sometimes, and very gracefully, these details are set to one side of the copy or are listed under the illustration for each item. These are layout considerations, however. The merchandise details must be included. Although to the novice they seem to intrude on the copy idea, in the hands of an experienced copywriter they slide right into place.

In any case, at this point, your body copy has been written and brought to a close.

Effective Retail Copy

How can you tell if it is good? What yardsticks do experts use to gauge whether the copy will be effective or not? After all, you cannot wait for next week's results to know whether to re-write today.

Well, first, let us say, unequivocally, that if you have not "re-written," do so at once, not only once, but twice or more. Re-write until you have satisfied what a famous advertising man called "that wee, small voice," and he added, "—don't ever be afraid of getting your hands dirty." [2] Regretfully, only the novice or student keeps a clean waste basket. The rest of us fill the waste basket with our *own* rejected drafts.

It is important to cultivate an objectivity about one's own output. So to "self-edit" is not to "self-destruct." On the contrary, it can save and eventually enhance one's ego. When you know in advance that you have trained your judgment for your own writing as well as for others, you can rationally accept or reject external criticism. This trait does not come all at once. External criticism, helpful but firm, is part of the young writer's training.

Now back to the criteria and guidelines. Any book on advertising, including this one, will tell you that there are no exact standards by which one can pre-test copy. But experience and some research have established certain guides that appear to result in effective copy. Remember once again, *effective copy (or advertising) is copy which in the end-result achieves its objective*, whether that be to create awareness, to build traffic, to sell a certain number of units, or any other feasible goal. Having said that, here are some criteria:

Honesty, Sincerity, Believability.   Copy must be honest. That is, it must tell the truth about goods and services. But that is not enough. It must be presented sincerely, so that the message (of true facts) it conveys will be believed. Put this way, it is hoped that it will be easily apparent that to make a true statement that no one believes certainly does not do the store any good at all.

Informative and Explicit   Copy as a whole and in its details must inform the potential customer, letting him know as much as possible about the product. This helps the retail advertiser. It helps the consumer to find good, sound reasons to buy. It is the copywriter's job to motivate the consumer by explicit, clear-cut, open statements about a product or service.

Simple yet Vivid Vocabulary.   Closely allied to the above guidelines is the use of simple language. By this we mean, not the common or vulgar, but the straightforward, uncomplicated language that we can all understand. The most intellectual of your audience does not approach your copy with dictionary in hand.

Always choose to use short sentences. Always select one- or two-syllable words in preference to the polysyllables.

Enrich your vocabulary, not by adding long words, but by adding vivid language for your writing. Get to know several words with similar meanings, and then train yourself to understand the shades of difference among them. These color your writing and help you to say precisely what you mean, *not almost* what you mean.

Words that describe texture, color, styles, line, whether of furniture or of apparel, must create pictures in the mind of the reader. Later, in the discussion of radio script-writing, we will find that words that form pictures double in importance for the copywriter.

It is not necessary to avoid totally current slang in retail advertising (as may be desirable in long-term national advertising). Retail advertising has an immediacy, a speed of preparation that makes it safe in terms of time-lapse. But use slang with the utmost care. Sometimes it fits. Be sure you know the current language you are attempting to use. Be careful not to be trailing two months behind with a phrase that is no longer used in the very circles you are trying to reach. Be sure your audience will accept this current usage.

Young people tend to picture all advertising as having been written, if not by greybeards, at least by those over thirty. With this in mind, they hate to read copy filled with an imitation of their own special language. They feel the writer is talking down to them, and they are sure he is misusing their words. Even if you, the young writer, are a lucky "under 30," remember the principle of believability mentioned above. Write clear, simple English, using words that make the right picture, and your audience, whether happy 18-year-olds or groaning 38's, will get your message.

Interesting, Enthusiastic. Copywriters cannot stay long at their jobs if they are bored. They are, generally, among the interested and interesting people with whom to talk. Few of them are bored with their jobs or the products about which they write. Therefore, it should be easy for them to write copy that is interesting and enthusiastic. "Easy" is not the case. It is one thing to feel, another to convey the excitement over a new product or one long in the store, or over a new department opening. Nevertheless, the copywriter, maintaining a natural and simple style, must instill this enthusiasm into the copy. "Gushing" is out. Cutesy-pie words are absolutely out. But honest delight in what you are writing about is most certainly in.

Persuasive. Copy has an objective to achieve, and it must persuade the reader or listener on its own. It can do this if it conveys conviction and believability. In observing the steps by which a potential customer is led to take positive action, a discussion that came very early in planning (Ch. 8), conviction was a most important step. It is this point that the consumer reaches through the persuasiveness of the copy.

Memorability, Identification. Finally, advertising must leave a clear impression not only of the merchandise offered but of the store and store-name that is offering it. The retail store must build a real identity in and through its advertising. The artwork plays a large part in this particular criterion of effective advertising. In fact, this is one guideline that depends upon the *whole* advertisement rather than the copy or the artwork alone. The total configuration carries the responsibility for the indelible memorability the store can hope to achieve in the minds of the potential customers.

Logotype or Signature

One of the final ingredients of the copy helps to stamp the impression of the identity of the store upon the consumer.

The logotype is the legal signature of the store. It is a professional word, often shortened to "logo." It is not used by the consumer. He uses "store name" or "signature." "Once upon a time," a

ILLUSTRATION 21   Variations in Logotype

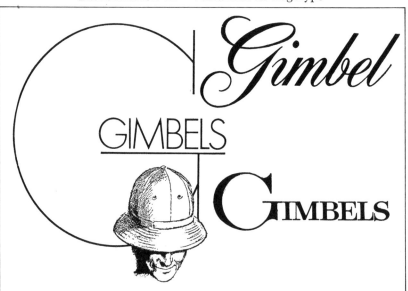

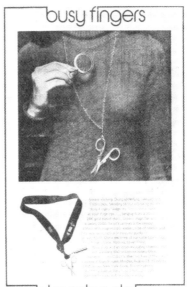

ILLUSTRATION 22
Variations in Logotype

store wrote or printed its name in just one way—in a script of a specially selected and distinctive type style. That "style" appeared in every advertisement, on every box, bag, in every window, on the store front, and so on.

Very recently, however, there has been a surprising change taking place. It has hit several stores simultaneously. Of course, we use the word "hit" somewhat humorously. Actually each store must have a considered policy—about the old way or the new. In the new way, many of our largest stores now exhibit a variety of signatures. One store will show its name in script, or in variety of script, and in some type style, or sometimes more than one type-style. Block letters, thin line letters—a whole variety of signature styles has appeared for any given store.

Some examples of Gimbels logotypes are included to indicate clearly what is meant (Ill. 21).

The policy behind this variety is not hard to understand. Large stores do not represent one image to all customers. They do not carry one kind of merchandise. Then why not match the art-style of the signature to the spirit of the merchandise and to the taste of the customer sought for that item or group of items?

Is this a wise move? Probably, given the current mood and times, it is. Our parents and grandparents wanted the security of the immovable, the inflexible, the "always there" sameness of one single signature or logotype everywhere, every time. But in our fluid society, individuality counts for more. The feeling of "this is for *me*" is more important than "this has always been there."

The customer's own interests change as she moves from the furniture department to apparel to a perfume boutique all within a single store. So, too, as her eye wanders through the advertisements in a single edition of (for example) a Sunday newspaper, she may perhaps be especially attracted by the lazy scrawl of a script signature for a beachwear advertisement, and then again drawn to the solid, heavier block letters for furniture copy.

Certainly, the differences are being noticed by the consumer and talked about. The phenomenon of the 60's and 70's, the shopping bag, is a most conspicuous place for the logotype of the store. People can be heard on buses and in clusters, saying "Oh, (store name) has a new shopping bag. They sign their name a new way."

If the reader thinks this is a conversation that will never get off this page, let us reassure him that it is real. People seem to like the change-over.

It must be emphasized at the same time that there are equally great stores all over the country who plan, style, and then hold on to one signature as their logotype. Over the decades, there may be subtle changes that a professional, matching advertisement against advertisement, can detect. Nonetheless, to the consumer's eye, the logotype remains the same.

However the store decides to handle it, the store name must be in every advertisement, on every bag or box, and in the store in numerous other places: on the top of menu cards, certainly on fashion-show programs, on private-brand merchandise, and any other spots that can carry it gracefully. An outstanding example is the newly-created logotype for Bloomingdale's, New York. In connection with their 100th Anniversary, this promotion-minded store had their advertising and, of course, their store signature redesigned. The new logotype appears in every place where a store name can be expected to be found. In the advertisements it is big, small, light and feminine or bold and masculine to fit the immediate need (Ill. 22).

There used to be talk, too, of advertising layout and typography so distinctive (and so much the same, day after day) that copy and artwork could appear in the newspaper without the store logo and all would recognize it for that store's advertising. This author's only answer to that is: "Don't bet on it!" The average consumer is not as interested in us as we are in ourselves. The newspapers are full of good-looking, well-put-together advertisements, and the *signature* is the one sure, clear-cut, unmistakable identifying symbol. Use it well and dramatically, but use it! Anything else is a costly mistake.

Store Information

A final "final" paragraph or two should be devoted to what is usually called "store information." In most cases, this refers to data about the store's address, its branches, its business hours, and telephone numbers. Sometimes it also includes mail-order information, delivery charges, and so forth.

This is important information for the customer. Possibly the most interesting to the customer is store hours. Stores vary, one from another, in their hours for opening and closing. The same store will vary from one day of the week to the next, and the next after that. Furthermore, all stores change their hours for holidays, and unquestionably change for pre-Christmas selling.

While the store information cannot, by any stretch of the imagination, be considered "creative" copy, it must be the responsibility of the copywriter.

Most copywriters keep on hand a supply of current store information, already set in type and cut out of current advertisement. As they finish a piece of copy, they can paste or tape down a small block of pre-set copy giving store information. They must, of course, make certain that the information is current and exactly what this advertisement calls for. This practice not only saves work but insures correct details in the block of copy, since it has already been set in type.

With this, we bring to a close a detailed analysis of the writing of print copy with its headlines, body copy, closing, signature, and store information.

FOOTNOTES

[1] Milton, *Advertising Copywriting*. Oceana Publications, Dobbs Ferry, 1969, *Grammatical* classification: statement, question, command. *Functional* classification: information, selective, advice or promise, claim, logo, mood-setting, provocative.

[2] Leo Burnett, "Keep listening to that Wee, Small Voice," *Readings in Advertising and Promotion Strategy*, Arnold M. Barban and C. H. Sandage. Richard D. Irwin, Inc., Illinois, 1968, pg. 162.

16

BROADCAST ADVERTISING COPY

This chapter, which will cover radio and television copy, can devote itself to the craftsmanship alone. Everything that has been said to be important to the copywriter in getting ready to write print copy applies here. The store and its departments, the product, the customer, and objectives are again focal areas for study.

But now with the merchandise again in front of him, the copywriter has been assigned to write for radio or perhaps for television. In a small store, if these media are used, this will certainly happen. Very likely, too, in a large store, the copywriter will be writing radio copy. It is possible that an agency will be called in for the television work, but perhaps not.

Radio Copy

Radio commercials are the most difficult of all advertising copy to write. Radio is a medium that reaches its audience through only one of the five senses: hearing, sound. It reaches the audience in the most fluid way of all.

The message is heard or it is missed. If it is missed it cannot be recaptured at will. In a newspaper or magazine, while there is admittedly only one sense (sight) that is called upon, yet the potential customer can turn back to the pages, can thumb through again, and so on.

Because of this, one must put oneself in a different frame of mind to write radio copy. The writer must keep in mind, as has been said earlier, that radio is a personal medium and must talk one-to-one to be effective. Therefore, your commercial message can be, in fact must be, informal, personal, warm, conversational, friendly. Here is the place for the dialogue between two friends about a product, between a mother and daughter about a sale. Here is the place for a monologue, a friendly recital of the values your store offers. The written form is that of an actor's script. (Fig. 16.)

The "spokesman," referred to in Copy Approaches in the previous chapter, would work very well in a continued series of commercials. The voice, as well as the name, would come to be known and trusted.

Music, jingles, sound effects add immeasurable "plus" qualities to your message. They alert the audience to listen to the com-

FIG. 16   BLANK RADIO SCRIPT SHEET

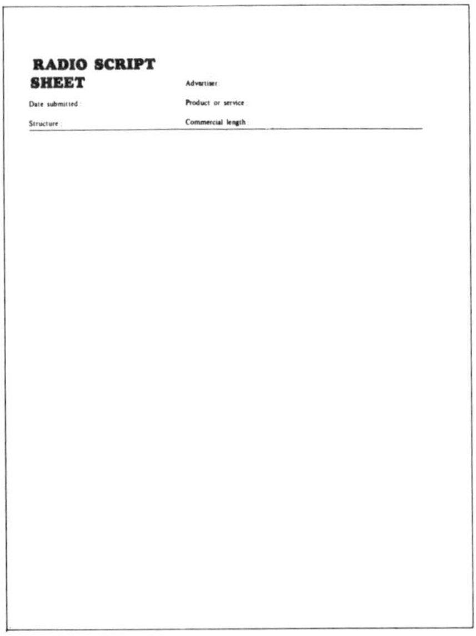

RADIO SCRIPT SHEET

Advertiser

Date submitted

Product or service

Structure

Commercial length

mercial. They can create a mood, make a slogan memorable, keep the listener interested to the end.

Remember, however, that out of those "plus" qualities comes high cost. Remember that retail radio copy should be changed as often as newspaper copy. An expert copywriter will, therefore, never recommend expensive music as background. Only if the copy strategy calls for a musical motif, as a sound-mark for the store itself, should the commercial call for *special* music, and, consequently, *special* expenditure. In this case, where it becomes the sound-mark of the store, it will be used time after time as a distinctive sound of your store, and will be worth its cost.

Sound can be classified (and what is said here applies to television as well). In sound, we have the spoken word, sound effects (indicated within the script as SFX), and music. The last two need some further clarification.

Sound effects on pre-recorded tape can be ordered through the recording studio. They can, of course, include every conceivable sound whether obvious like a fire-engine siren or subtle like a breeze among leaves. The sounds of a city or of a roaring ocean shore can be incorporated into a script and a sound track will be available.

Music, also, exists for your use. The least expensive is music in public domain; *i.e.*, music whose copyright has run out, and which you are consequently free to use. "Free to use" means that the score is free of charge. You may very likely find you need to have it arranged for your purpose (that costs money—see the next paragraph or so). The use of classic or of turn-of-the-century tunes like "Bicycle Built for Two" is in this category.

Second, we come to another kind of music that already exists. That is current music under full copyright. TWA's use several years ago of "Up, Up and Away" is an example. Where you wish to use current music, you must expect to pay a considerable sum for the rights, the sum depending upon the current popularity of the song, its composer, and the group associated with its playing. This kind of music certainly would not seem to be advisable for a retailer—unless the circumstances were so pat, so appropriate that it was felt it was a "must" at any cost.

Then there is music that does *not* exist until the advertiser (through his writers) creates it. Here, the copywriter works with the musical arranger to create words and a tune to go with them. This is often called a "musical jingle." This procedure is not inexpensive, but if it can express the whole significance of a store and is expected to be used over a long, long period of time, it is certainly worth the cost. This is very much like institutional advertising. However brief a part the jingle may play in each individual commercial, it can become an important sound-mark, the store's trademark in music.

It is important, next, to keep in mind that commercials are at most 60 seconds, frequently 30 seconds, and sometimes 10 seconds in length. Even if you take the longest time, you must (in 60 seconds) catch your audience's attention, get them to listen, instill your message about your store and product into the heads of potential customers, making an impression that will create conviction and action. Those impressions frequently cannot be acted upon at once, but must be carried in the listener's mind to be acted upon later.

Some suggestions then become clear:

1. Call attention to your message first, *then* give the message.
2. Use music or sound effects like a headline to command attention, select an audience by its own character, and interest that audience enough to continue to listen.
3. The body of the script must feature *one* product benefit and only one. Small merchandise features that help to define a product may be given, but remember, for most people, the ear alone does not carry as impressive a message to the brain as does the eye, or the ear and the eye. Details tend to fade out. So, to repeat, select a strong product benefit and stay with that one benefit.
4. In the time alloted to you, repeat your major product and its benefit or selling point.
5. Give your store name near the beginning and repeat it again at the end of the commercial. If address and phone number are called for, and in retail advertising they usually are, give them and repeat them at the end. If phone orders are important, repeat the phone number twice.

6.   Read your copy out loud. This is a must. However low you keep your voice (and you are reading to yourself), do not omit this. Do it consciously until it becomes habit. There are two reasons for this: *First,* it helps the writer to avoid tongue-twisters which can spoil the best announcer's delivery of your message. It helps avoid ugly, harsh sounds, too many "s" sounds, which give a hissing effect. *Second,* it enables you to use a stop-watch (or sweep second hand) to time your own commercial. This is important, if your message is not to be cut off the air before it has been completed.

7.   Timing is important enough to merit its own paragraph. Under-write, do not over-write. If you are writing for a taped spot, your studio will force you to the right time, if you have been careless. But if you are writing for live commercials, the station will just cut your announcer off the air. While speech rate varies, two words per second gives good delivery. You may not agree and want your copy read faster. If so, instruct the announcer at the bottom of your script-page. Thus, for a 60-second spot, do not write more than 120 words; less is better. For a 30-second commercial 58 to 60 words, and so on.

8.   Keep your "cast of characters" small. Sixty seconds on radio will not generally permit or call for a Shakespearean drama.

9.   The same is true of music. If the decision is made to use music, keep it simple. It will help the memorability, which is a prime function of the music you use.

In radio (and in television) the copywriter must know more than he perhaps expected of production, its needs and problems. The copywriter in this field does *not* need to be a sound or camera technician, but he must be aware of the cost involved and how radio commercials may be produced at low cost.

If time is bought on a station for general broadcast, there will be needed either a *live* or a *taped* commercial, or a combination of both.

A *live* commercial as its name implies is a selling message delivered by an actual announcer so that the listening audience at home hears what is being said at the time it is broadcast.

A *taped* commercial is produced electronically (and is referred to as an E.T., electronic transcription) at a studio with a chosen announcer, and with any musicians, vocalists, or other personnel the copywriter has written into the script. This is produced on a master tape and additional tapes are reproduced to be sent to the specified stations to be put on the air in the time slots bought. Sometimes, stations will require records, or "platters," instead of tapes.

Clearly, for a retailer, the live announcement has the greatest advantages.

1.   There is no production cost, whatsoever.

2.   It is quick, current, and immediate.

3.   It can be changed in an emergency in almost no time. (While the station would accept this only in a *real* emergency, it can be done.)

4.   Since a retail store wants new copy for each commercial, live announcements produce just that: fresh, new copy at the store's will.

5.   Retailers, even larger stores, are basically localized in an area that can be covered by a few stations, and the very preparation of a master tape, where there is no need to reproduce it in reasonable quantity, would be an unjustified expense.

6.   The retail store, as a local merchant, can capitalize on the warmth and familiarity of the local announcer, whose voice is undoubtedly recognized by his listeners.

Taped commercials work much better for a national advertiser or for a giant retail firm which wants to air commercials across the country or part of the country. For that kind of advertiser the advantages of E.T.'s are clear:

1.   There is accurate duplication of their message over many, many stations.

2.   Their messages generally have several months of life and can be repeated again and again.

3.   Their variety comes through the rotation of several tapes, made at the same time in a studio, covering the same subject, in different versions.

4. If they have spent a lot of money on a musical arrangement, the tape provides a correct and acoustically satisfactory reproduction of that music.

The combination of live and taped messages provides just that. Frequently, there will be a musical introduction that is taped (and delivered to the radio station as a numbered and identified E.T.), and a message by a live announcer given right at the station at time of broadcast.

A retail store might very well use this combination, especially if it had planned and executed some motif-music. Then it would have the advantage of good reproduction of its music at studio quality and the current freshness of the live announcement.

There is a fourth method of getting a commercial message on the air. It is one that should be used if the advertising strategy has called for buying time on a "personality" show (a husband-wife team, a talk show, or a well-known disc jockey). In this case, the advertiser is best advised to make use of the station's personality, for which he has paid a premium price. This can be done through using, not a script, but a Copy Fact Sheet. This method lists the points you wish to make on behalf of your store and the merchandise in the store, sentence by sentence, separated and numbered. Every fact you can think of should be included. The rest is up to the "personality," who quite literally ad libs your commercial.

The advantages are these: Your store bought this kind of time at a premium because it wanted the voice, the mannerisms, the humor, the authority of the personality. All of these add to one thing that the personality has going for him: audience loyalty. Thus, you tie in to this loyalty when you let him (or her) say it his own way.

What are the disadvantages? They loom large—inaccuracy, mispronunciation, cynical humor, misplaced humor, even objectionable humor in today's spectrum—all of these are possible. Most d.j.'s have a "put-down" style of delivery, but the best ones are equal to the best of any group. They are professional, which means they know their business.

Add to the Copy Fact Sheet a line or two indicating *what your store expects* (or *will not accept*), and you will end up with a series of strong, varied commercials carrying the imprint of that personality's unique flavor. The end result will be to win *his* loyal audience and support for *your* store and its merchandise.

The foregoing covers the essentials for a young copywriter in the radio field. If it is carefully reviewed, a good basis for sound radio copy will emerge.

Television Copy

Someone writing about television commercials has said that they are, generally speaking, 60-second short stories. As such, like the little girl with the curl, when they are good they are very, very good, and when they are bad they are *horrid.*

But, on the whole, the best and the worst of television commercials are initiated and aired by national advertisers. Retail advertising, moving along into continually greater use of television, is generally hitting the middle of the road in its creative output.

Writing for time bought on local stations, the copywriter has an opportunity to tell about the store and its merchandise, to show what is important, and to show it in action. Whether it be the courteous service of a store in bringing parcels to a parked car, or new ways to tie fashion scarves, the copywriter can now show how it is, as well as tell it as it is. A good television script can bring together the best of the visibility of newspaper advertising with the best of the sound inherent in radio, and, in doing so, add a synergistic extra dimension.

Copywriting for television moves from an idea to sounds and pictures set up in script form (Fig. 17), then on to storyboard form (Fig. 18a, 18b) for translation into the actual commercial ready for broadcast.

Color television has become so commonplace that it must be a consideration for every large-size store located in the heavy marketing areas. For the smaller store, black and white represents a more feasible vehicle.

The large store is cited because of the high cost of color. The heavy market areas are specified because of the concentration of color sets in the households located in those areas. Thus, in many

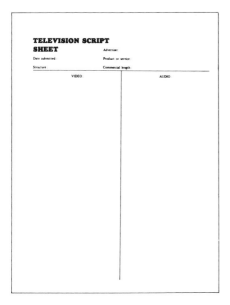

FIG. 17   BLANK TELEVISION SCRIPT SHEET

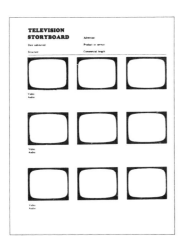

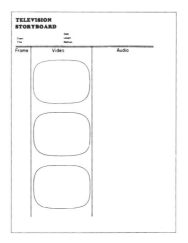

FIG. 18   EXAMPLES OF TELEVISION STORYBOARDS

cases, color is available to the copywriter and must be part of his thinking about his "Ad Factors" (see Ch. 14).

Demonstration has, since its beginning, been one of television's strongest points. Whether you think of demonstration as showing how to use a vegetable knife-and-curler, or more subtly, the heel-proof quality of the carpeting your store has to sell, *showing* is the dominant characteristic of TV. Obviously, then, whenever possible, the copywriter must take advantage of this asset.

The fluid, "here now, gone the next minute" quality exists in television as it does for radio. Especially for retail advertising, where frequent change is paramount, each commercial must catch and hold the attention of as many as possible of "real" potential customers among the viewing audience.

At this point, at the risk of being repetitious, we must again call the copywriter's attention to the consideration of the specific audience he wishes to reach with his store's message.

These messages can be heavily institutional. In this case, then, the *family*, rather than just mother *or* father *or* younger members, can be the target of the commercial. Through short spots that talk about the service, the quality, the reputation of the store, whether it be the local supermarket, drugstore, or apparel shop, an enduring impact can be made at an economical figure.

Supermarket chains, in 1972 and 1973 proliferated this kind of television commercial. Rightly so, for with the upswing of food prices, the food chains with the best foresight realized that it was important to address the family as a whole, including both the breadwinner and the housewife—each of whom had equal concern with what could be bought with the dollar. The institutional messages stated the chain's willingness to keep prices down as low as wholesale prices would permit, while stressing that they would maintain the service to which the shopper looks forward.

For the department store, large or small, strong institutional copy can be a very important portion of the total advertising plan. While constant repetition of the same message would not be desirable, some essential can be repeated again and again within different versions, with sound results.

Somehow the ear hears with pleasure the repetition of a known refrain, while the eye rejects and the mind is bored with the repetition of the same visual.

As in radio, therefore, a good musical introduction is worth searching for and paying for especially if the store has both a television and a radio schedule of respectable size. It can carry the weight of the store name both in institutional and in product advertising.

It must be borne in mind, however, that we are talking of 60- and 30-second commercials and sometimes 20- and 10-second slots. Consequently, when we talk of musical repetition or of a "sound mark," a few bars of music are all that can be included, at most.

A retail store can, however, produce commercials without music or sound effects and many do. Here the entire reliance is on the spoken word and the action that goes with it.

Since enough has been said in the radio section on music, this section will concentrate on the copy and action, the audio and the video that the copywriter prepares for the commercial.

The writer will do best to think of action that will demonstrate the best qualities of the merchandise to be advertised. Where the single dominant product benefit or selling point can be isolated, that ought to be demonstrated in a clear and interesting way. The video (what is seen) will then show the product in use or action. Audio (what is heard) will explain and underscore the benefits derived from the use and performance of the product.

This can be as appropriate for floor covering as for children's school apparel, or diving gear. It can be adapted for food, for tires, or for any other commodity sold by any retail store.

The audio and the video must perform several functions:

1. Mention and show the store name.
2. Indicate clearly the merchandise and demonstrate, while stating, its specific benefits, characteristics or quality.
3. State how to get the product: *i.e.* "Come in," "Phone," "Mail," etc.
4. Re-state and re-show the store name.
5. Clearly show (while saying) the address. Sometimes it is

necessary to give several addresses. These can be shown on the screen, while the voice makes a general statement, as, "At all branches."

6. Give and repeat the phone number.

While action is not only possible but desirable to show selling points or benefits, the audio must still carry the selling idea. It is important to consider what happens in a living room during a commercial. This need not be described too lengthily here. We are all people—as well as students of advertising. If too much dependence is placed upon the gimmicky idea of the silent screen—showing a beautiful use of the product while nothing is said—the message may be lost. How often have we, ourselves, not turned our backs to adjust a chair, to pick up a book, to go to the next room. The voice can still catch the audience, but the silent screen with its dramatic action is lost.

In fact, while creativity and originality must be the cutting edge of a commercial, it is important to remember that, again as has been said before, advertising is a selling tool, not a pure art form. The store and the merchandise are the focal point of the whole enterprise. State them, show them, repeat them. Don't lose sight of them, and don't let your audience lose sight *and* sound of them.

In a short, 10-second ID (identification spot) it may be possible only to show a background of the merchandise while stating the special selling point of the commercial, and then "super over" (superimpose) the same selling point. For example, this could be done for a carpet sale. In a short 10-second or 20-second commercial, all you can do is show either the rug or carpet laid down in a room or a department full of bright-colored, rolled-up carpeting, announce the special sale prices, super over the rug display a restatement of the sale prices, while holding the store name throughout. The end could be a notice of the date of the sale, a repeat of the name and address.

The copywriter must prepare a script that clearly states in the left column what is to be shown and gives camera directions. In the right-hand column are the directions for music, sound and speech, *and* the actual words to be spoken. (Fig. 17, page 165.)

For a formal, careful translation to a storyboard an art director will be called in, but the copywriter should be able to handle the storyboard form, using at least stick figures in the little frames to indicate a rough progression of action, while below each the audio and directions are given, with the actual words typed below that. Two types of generally used storyboards have already been pictured in this book (Figures 18a and 18b). The horizontal structure is most popular.

Because of the nature of the medium, sound is delayed, so that there are fewer seconds for your audio message than for the video that accompanies it. A reasonable guide may be the following:

Length of Time Slot	*Length of Video*	*Length of Audio*	*Approx. No. of Words* *
60 sec.	60	58	116–125
30	30	28	56– 63
20	20	18	36– 40
10 (ID-w. Station Break)	7¼	6	12– 15

* Based on 2 words a minute or a bit more. Obviously, number of words per commercial is meaningless when music and SFX are included.

Again as in radio, the copywriter must use a stop-watch to time his own work, but this time the secret whisperer must also become a secret actor. It is clearly worthless to time the audio alone. Action takes time and must be allowed for.

There are several approaches to the writing of a television commercial. A listing of these will afford the copywriter a structure on which to build his commercial message. Among these are:

The Narrative. This approach includes a small plot or story which can be developed as a fantasy, or as the "people next door," or the slice-of-life. It can be dramatized, too, as a Knight of the Round Table or a Castle in Spain. This approach can, of course, be serious, sophisticated, or humorous. In any of these variations, the reputation of the store, or the product benefit or selling point is embedded into a little story.

The Testimonial. This approach brings an outside, presumably objective and always approving, voice to the merchandise or the store as the subject. In its purest form, the "testimony" is given about the product itself.

The testimonial can also be given by an important personality whose reputation and position in another field entirely brings a sense of importance to the subject at hand. Criticism of this type of approach always rests on the use or non-use of the actual product. Where there is no indication that the personality does himself use the product, there is good reason for the public to feel cheated. A retail store should not make this mistake. Their wares are varied enough so that, if they decide to use an important personality to speak of a product, he can be and is really a user of that merchandise.

The spokesman is another version that has been roughly discussed in the section on copywriting for print (Ch. 15).

This entire approach, while useful for merchandise advertising, is especially well suited to institutional advertising on television.

Factual Presentation. This approach covers the straight news announcement of a sale, of an opening, of any store event. It is a way of conveying any information that should be given to the public.

Other forms can cross these basic lines. An institutional story can be told as a factual *history* or as a *documentary.*

Merchandise can be presented as a *solution to a problem* either factually or in the narrative approach.

Demonstrations can be coupled with a factual presentation or incorporated into a slice-of-life story.

In any case, special effects and even animation can add to the interest of the message.

Once again, as in the audio discussion of radio, a copywriter must keep some thought of budget in mind. And, in addition in television, he must think of action and cameramen as additional areas of expenditure.

Residuals

We cannot leave this area without some attention to a very specific area of expense in both radio and television planning. This item covers *residuals,* or talent re-use fees. Musicians, announcers, vocalists and actors are paid on a union scale under union contract agreements that stipulate how often a commercial may be replayed or re-used for a given fee. Generally, the first fee pays for the recording and production of the commercial and 13 weeks thereafter. At the end of this period (or whatever period is originally specified), each of the kinds of talent enumerated above receives a new fee, again for a given period of time. Moreover, each variation of the script within a campaign carries its own fee.

For a retail store, this does not present so great an item of expense. For a straight, live radio announcement none of this enters into the picture. But as soon as actors, musicians, vocalists, and announcers are used in taped or partially taped commercials, where obviously there will be repetition, residuals must be considered.

This then adds still another reason for the copywriter to have more than a little knowledge of how commercials are produced.

17

VISUAL ELEMENTS
OF THE WHOLE ADVERTISEMENT

As we come to the last of the creative elements, we could start the chapter with an argument. What is the visual element? Is it the graphics, the layout, the artwork, or the typographical style? Or, in a sense, isn't it the entire print advertisement as a whole?

The reader of a publication, newspaper or magazine, looks at the page or fractional-page of advertising. He sees a photo or a sketch or both. He sees type: some large, some smaller, some tiny. Sometimes he sees some intertwined initials or some abstract art. And all of this has been set into a predetermined space taken (paid for) by the advertiser.

The eye rightly picks up the *whole*. If some element catches the attention, the mind begins to separate the elements out of the whole, to look at and judge the artwork in a subjective and general way (not usually as "art"); then to read the copy, and to note the store name. Of course, the process is lightning-fast, but that does not change the essential sequence.

The visual plays a vital role in the selling process and the selling power of a print advertisement, as it does, of course, in a television commercial. Here, however, we will deal solely with the print visual.

Let us start then with the total configuration, the whole advertisement. Visual impact is based on:

1. *Layout* — the way the artist planned to place type, copy, artwork, and logotype within the allotted area of white space.
2. *Artwork* — the photograph, illustration or, in some cases, abstract art decoration called for by the art director
3. *Lettering* — the hand reproduction of copy that could be set in type.
4. *Typography* —- the style of type chosen and the variations in sizes determined by the art director.
5. *Color* — particularly important, in retail advertising, for newspaper advertising wherever the opportunity is given to use this tool.

Of these elements, numbers 1, 2, and 4 are always present. Numbers 3 and 5 are options. But these are the elements that create the *visual* attention value on the printed page.

Layout

The pleasing arrangement of artwork and type within a given area is, in itself, an art and a skill. In itself, it has manipulative power in catching attention and creating interest. It has an immediately understood character.

Certainly, any reader of a publication, even if he is uninterested in advertising techniques, would immediately recognize the upper-class quality of a store from an advertisement with lots of white space.[1] Conversely, he would detect a discount operation from a cluttered, "busy" layout.

There is no question that white space is pleasing to the eye. Yet, the character of a given store may demand, through its own heavily laden counters, packed racks, masses of promotional signs, that the newspaper advertisement be equally busy. Then a crowded layout would be appropriate and in keeping with its function of representing a true image of the store itself.

To answer a perhaps unspoken question, in magazines and less frequently in newspapers, the background may sometimes be reversed, so that the reader sees it as black or grey, with the type in white. While some testing indicates that white on black loses readership, many fashion advertisers believe it looks smart or chic and use it anyway. The background in the layout stage is still spoken of as "white space." The reversing takes place in the engraving stage. (See Ill. 23.)

There are styles in layouts, and some fads. Today, one of the best new styles is the use of solid masses set closely together with lots of white space surrounding them. (See Ills. 24 and 25.)

ILLUSTRATION 23   Reverse Plate Ad

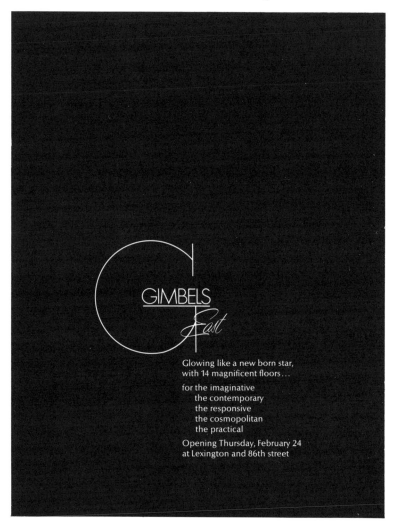

ILLUSTRATION 24
Good Newspaper Layout

Another current style in layout is the use of informally balanced elements in the space, as opposed to formal pairing of left and right sides. (See Fig. 19 and 20 and Ill. 26 and 27.)

FIG. 19   FORMAL BALANCE

FIG. 20   INFORMAL BALANCE

Informal Balance within the space provides an opportunity to allow for large areas of white space, and adds a dash, a dramatic look to the whole. It is particularly successful in high-fashion or limited fashion advertising. (It is to be noted that in the sense in which this author uses the term "high or limited fashion," it can refer to the top-level automobile line, to liquor, travel, hotels. It need not, should not, be confined to apparel.) Numerically, however, there are as many formally as informally balanced layouts to be found in any category.

For many years, Art Directors followed the artist's rule of placing the point of prominent focal attention at a point $\frac{5}{8}$ up the page space. Gaze Motion is then created by the placement of the other

ILLUSTRATION 25   Good Layout "Gone Wrong"

400

When we added up the combined experience of our furniture and decorating experts, it came to almost 400 years and that's like 400 reasons why we say we're not a store but a showroom . . . serving you with specialists, not just clerks.

You get hard facts, not hard sell, when we guide you through our 4 spacious showroom floors of period

and contemporary furniture displays. We know our stock and we understand your needs. We've been giving personalized, attentive showroomstyle service for so long, we wouldn't know how to do otherwise. We are dedicated to the idea that you must be satisfied. And you'll be more than satisfied by our attractive special showroom prices.

Come in for a new experience in showroom shopping . . . showroom style!

ILLUSTRATION 26
Layout: Formal Balance

ILLUSTRATION 27
Layout: Informal Balance

ILLUSTRATION 28   Layout: Gaze
Motion—Focal Point
⅝ Vertically on Page

elements, artwork and type, so that the eye moves easily, as if
guided from most important Point #1 to Point #2 to Point #3,
and so on.

For example, in the Saks-Fifth Avenue advertisement (Ill. 28),
the eye should "hit the page" on the model's head and the line,
"Where's the blaze?" Then it should move to the neckline of the
shirt, down the stripes, to the copy block, and then to the logotype.

This is "classic," because it is natural and has been the pattern
for a long time. Another successful advertisement, with good gaze
motion, is included (Ill. 29).

ILLUSTRATION 29
Layout: Good Gaze Motion—
Focal Point as Expected

The fad for tricky layouts plays havoc with this rule. Whenever you break a rule, you must be doubly sure of what effect the new way will have. It can have stunning impact (Ill. 30), or it can be weak and easy to pass by (Ill. 31).

ILLUSTRATION 30
Layout: Successful Focal
Point out of Expected Place

ILLUSTRATION 31   Poor Gaze Motion

Another classic pattern for large stores is to employ a single style of layout that will, with only minor changes, be used for all its advertising. Today's usage among some stores dictates a wide range of layout, not a single layout-style.

Within the widest latitude of layout, however, what almost invariably remains unchanged for a given store is the proportion of white space. This, then, is the decisive factor in the atmosphere that a layout builds. Whichever way it is handled, layout may be said to be the "packaging" of the advertisement.

Artwork: Photography, Illustration

As was mentioned in the section on headlines (Ch. 15), the artwork? It is a generic name given to the graphic visual on the page. It may be:

1. Photography
2. Illustration (or sketch)
3. Decorative elements (designs).

As was mentioned in the section on headlines (Ch. 15), the artwork shares the headline's function of capturing that first attention. Especially for today's consumers, with their quick reaction to what is pictured (as opposed to the printed word), the artwork may carry the greatest responsibility as an attention-getter among the elements of a print advertisement.

Next, the artwork naturally illustrates the product or merchandise. It can emphasize special details. It can show the merchandise being used in an appropriate setting. It can illustrate a service offered, also.

Third, the artwork can create an atmosphere for the product or the store. This function, of course, is all-important to institutional advertising.

Fourth, the artwork can glamorize the merchandise. It is hoped that it does this honestly, through the charm and pleasing effect of the sketch or photograph. It would not be acceptable (neither honest nor believable) to enhance the product by drawing some detail or portion in an extreme way. Some drawings of automobiles, for example, exaggerate a car's length unrealistically.

Fifth, the art director can use the artwork to emphasize important points in the selling message.

Finally, artwork is an essential part of the gaze motion discussed earlier as an element of layout. It leads the eye the way the creator of the advertisement wants it to go.

Shall a store use photography or illustration? Here again, as so often before, there are (a), (b), and (a plus b). Most stores adopt one art style for newspapers and, if they advertise in magazine, a format for that medium. But some stores, some of our largest, use both photos and sketches.

What are the characteristics of each? Can they be said to have advantages, disadvantages?

First, the most practical guide of all is the kind of stock (paper) that is used by the medium. The coated-stock, glossy magazine paper gives good reproduction of photography detail. The dull, more absorbent newspaper stock does not.

Most magazines use glossy paper. Some of the more lurid use a dull, grainy paper. (In fact, magazines are sometimes talked of in journalese as the "slicks" and the "pulps.") So on the coated stock of the magazines, if that is your medium, either photography or illustration will yield good results.

In the newspaper field, there is a greater usage today of printing by offset on semi-smooth stock that corrects many of the flaws of reproducing photography on the usual news stock. Otherwise, the big-city dailies still use the familiar coarse-grain newspaper stock.

(The reason for good and bad reproduction will be discussed further in Chapter 19 on print production. Loosely, it has to do with need for heavy black inking and the consequent smudging and filling up of what should be light or white areas.)

So the art director has one guideline in his choice: quality of reproduction. It is interesting to note, however, that good results can be obtained despite all that has been said. (See Ill. 32.)

The overall advertising policy and advertising objectives of the store are probably equally strong determinants. Based upon the personality of the store, the advertising policy has been set with long-range objectives. The artwork is an important element, of course, in conveying the image of the store. Generally, today, the stores which have a reputation for high quality project this

ILLUSTRATION 32   Good Photography in Newspaper

through illustrations. Illustrations permit an aura of elegance in the very style of the drawing. Furthermore, a background may be sketched in. A model may be imagined and drawn with just the neckline (long), the wristbones (delicate), the legs (long and slim) to convey the air that is wanted. A gamin, young-girl look, or a worldly sophisticated look can be projected by the skilled artist-illustrator.

Photography, while it can be tremendously dramatic when well reproduced, loses in reproduction in a newspaper. This has already been pointed out. It tends to blur out, to lose sharpness and drama. It does, on the other hand, preserve its own special characteristic of realism. Many discount and volume stores use photography to enhance their store's reputation for low prices. The realism of the photograph tends to say to the customer, "Look, we have nothing to hide. You can see for yourself every detail of these furniture pieces, of this three-piece suit." This reinforces the message of low prices for equal quality.

The above statement mentions the realism of photography. Over and above store policy or objectives, whenever a product calls for an exact reproduction, either because of its complexity, its newness, or some other special attribute, photography should be used to convey that kind of visual imprint.

Finally, there is the question of emphasis. An Art Director can call for special emphasis (*not distortion*) in an advertisement for a household appliance or household furnishings or a man's suit. When he wants this, he is probably better advised to use a sketch than a photograph. A detail can be highlighted by the illustrator more easily and more clearly. Remembering always that we are talking of newspaper advertising and reproduction, let us take an example. If the fit of the collar and shoulders of a man's suit is an especially notable point to be emphasized in the newspaper advertisement, photography would need several shots to do the job. There would be a shot of the man in the suit, and a close-up of the collar and shoulders. Another possibility would present the second shot in a close-up under a magnifying glass. This would be a good way to handle an interesting stitching pattern, but awkward otherwise.

In illustration, on the other hand, the artist, with proper direction from the Art Director, highlights the desired area right in the sketch. For simpler, more direct effects, illustration emphasizes best.

Classifications for Reproduction

While production will be discussed in a later chapter, some preview is necessary here as to the types of artwork, in accordance with the way they will be engraved or otherwise reproduced.

The Art Director may use line drawings or half-tones. The line drawing is composed of sharp black lines on white. Some thickness can be produced by thick black lines. But, in a line drawing (called a "line cut") there will be no gradation of depth of blackness.

In half-tone art (wash drawings and photography), the artwork has black and white, but also has many *tones* of grey.

In the interest of economy, a very popular compromise for achieving a tone-effect in the printed advertisement is the use of a line drawing with a Ben Day screen. The Ben Day screen provides a variety of dots on a transparent sheet or screen laid over the drawing itself or a zinc plate of the drawing. Then the two (original line drawing and screen) are shot together, and the eye picks up the holes in the inked screen as shading.

Various screens provide varying densities of dots per square inch. Once again, the coarseness of the newspaper stock limits the fineness of the screen to a half-dozen or so among the many gradations that are available. Too fine a screen in newspaper printing would "pile up" ink spots too close together with a resultant smudge.

Wash drawings are generally now highlight-dropout drawings where the artist uses a chemical instead of water. This results is clear white areas (the "dropout") wherever the artist would like that effect.

Finally, the photograph always calls for a half-tone engraving. Lights and shadows produce the greys of the finally reproduced artwork.

As to costs, medium and large stores have fully staffed advertising departments with an Art Director and some artist personnel on salary, for layout and sketching. A number of them, not too many, have finishing artists or illustrators, too. Fewer have photographers who are salaried and on staff. Whichever is the practice in a given store, there is a trend toward equalizing the prices of good illustrations with good photographs.

On the other hand, many stores' advertising departments bring their artwork through the stages of comprehensive layout, and then call in an outside artist or photographer.

These outside people may work through an art agency. Yet, often, they work on their own directly and closely with the store and the Art Director, who uses their services over and over again. This is to be expected, for these free-lance artists and photographers develop a reputation for their own style. Often they specialize in one kind of work, children for example, hard goods, high fashion, foods, and so on.

It is to the Art Director's advantage to use various artists in their own specialized fields over and over, so that, for example, his store's children's-wear advertising art always has the same look. This is equally true of photography, where the Art Director will probably work steadily with one or two free-lance photographers and may even stipulate the same model.

In the case of free-lance work, again the cost tends to even out, so that cost itself should not be a factor in the decision to use illustration vs. photography.

Lettering

Finally, within the structure of artwork, a word or two must be included about lettering. The word is clear enough, it would seem. Again, in keeping with the kind of store for which you are working, you must give consideration to the possibility of hand-lettering sometimes the logotype, sometimes the headings of copy blocks, sometimes the entire headline.

It would be foolhardy to attempt to say that lettering does one thing or another. It completes the advertisement artistically, if the advertisement was so planned. It can be blocky and bold, or graceful and elegant. It is always, however, individual, and lends distinctiveness to a store's advertising.

Typography

Typography is an important concern of the Art Director and Production Manager in the production stage of the advertisement. The selection of a type face (a style), however, is a high-level art decision to be made in cooperation with the Advertising Manager.

While type itself is a vehicle used to convey the printed selling message, it is, because of its great variety, far more than just that.

A *type face* is a design made distinctive by many factors in the formation of the characters, letters of the alphabet and numerals. Type faces have been given names frequently for the designer of the face, as Bodoni, Goudy. Other names are descriptive, as Bank Script, Brush, and so forth.

There are many ways of classifying type. The variety, as has been noted, is so great that it would be possible to make a lifetime study of the field. Fine typographers are themselves artists and deserve the respect they command.

Type can be classified into two groups (see Fig. 21): sans serifs and serifs, which can be further classified into families; for our purposes, we need not go far, especially since there is more than one system of classification in use. Serifs are the small projections coming off the main stroke of a letter; they are actually an outgrowth of Roman stonecutters' way of initiating a letterform in stone by cutting out a wedge-shape at the top and bottom of the stroke. Sans serif type is without such projections. The type you are reading is serif-ed; the type in the figures in this book is sans serif.

FIG. 21   EXAMPLES OF SERIF AND SANS SERIF TYPEFACES

Italian Old Style   Serif type faces

The Times New Roman Italic

Helvetica   Sans serif type faces

Gothic Extra Condensed No. 2

Serif faces, first developed in imitation of hand-lettered faces formed with a broadedged pen, had not only serifs but also had thicker and thinner parts in each letter. At first, technology limited what the type founder/designer (they were then the same) could do, so the type of those days—early 1600's—had sturdy serifs, marked diagonal stress, and a not very marked difference between thicks and thins. Nowadays this family is called *Old Style*, although the men who were its creators did not know it would be. Technology advanced and type began to show crisper serifs, greater contrast between thicks and thins and a more vertical stress. Because these typefaces bridged the Old Style with the Modern, they were called *Transitional*—around 1750. In *Modern* faces, in the early 1800's, these refinements culminated in slender, completely horizontal bar serifs, very pronounced thicks and hairline thins, and a totally vertical stress. As you can see, here Modern doesn't mean the latest type style. (See Fig. 22).

Sans serif types appeared first in the mid-1800's and were called *gothics* or *grotesks*; they still are in some instances. They have no stress at all because the letters are all the same width. Of course they have no serifs.

After the mid 1800's, type design became quite unrestrained and everything was tried: expanding, condensing, shadowing, crosshatching, curlicueing, making serifs into slabs, imitating typewriters, handwritten scripts, etc.—so that some types cannot be classified as other than *Miscellaneous*, although within this category there are recognizable sub-groups.[1]

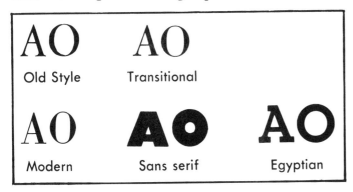

FIG. 22   PROGRESSION OF TYPE FAMILIES

CHARACTERS IN FONT IN EACH SIZE	CHARACTERS IN FONT IN EACH SIZE
ABCDEFGHIJKLMNOP QRSTUVWXYZ& ABCDEFGHIJKLMNOPQRSTUVWXYZ& abcdefghijklmnopqrstuvwxyz fi fl ff ffi ffl $1234567890 ., : ; - ! ? '' ( ) [ ] % * † ‡ § ¶ - — ⅛ ¼ ⅜ ½ ⅝ ¾ ⅞ •	ABCDEFGHIJKLMNOP QRSTUVWXYZ& abcdefghijklmnopqrstuvwxyz fi fl ff ffi ffl $1234567890 , . : ; - ! ? '' ( ) { } % * † ‡ § ¶ - — ⅛ ¼ ⅜ ½ ⅝ ¾ ⅞ •

FIG. 23   TWO COMPLETE TYPE FONTS

Within a *font*, there will be numerals, punctuation, and an alphabet in upper case (capitals) and in lower case. Additionally, in some type faces there are small-sized capitals. Examples of full fonts are shown in Fig. 23.

In a *type series*, there may be a variety of weights, which appear on the printed pages as gradations from a light, delicate, and slender stroke to a heavy, black, bulky stroke. All of these, it must be clear, are still the same single type-face design. In other words, the distinctive quality of the face remains unchanged throughout all weight variations. (See Fig. 24.)

FIG. 24   EXAMPLE OF A TYPE SERIES

Venus Light	Venus Light Extended
Venus Medium	Venus Medium Ext'd
Venus Bold	**Venus Bold Ext'd**
Venus Extrabold	**Venus Extrabold Ext'd**
Venus Light Italic	Venus Light Condensed
Venus Medium Italic	VENUS BOLD COND.
Venus Bold Italic	VENUS EXTRABOLD COND.

FIG. 25   EXAMPLES OF VERY DIFFERENT TYPE STYLES

Type faces should be selected with care, with an eye to long-term, if not permanent, use by a store. Legibility is, far and above all others, the primary consideration. Consequently, the headline with its large size need not be the same type face as the body copy. Figure 25, above, shows a variety of different, more and less legible, types.

Type is divided into *text* or *body copy*, in which the bulk of a book or brochure is set (you are now reading body copy); and *display copy* which is the heading or large type at the top of an announcement or the title page of a book. The body copy is normally set in 12- or 14-point type and must be easily readable. Type faces are measured in points, with 72 points to an inch. This measurement refers to the vertical height of the shoulder, the metal on which the letter lies, raised. Display or headline type is usually at least 18 pt.; body copy, as noted 12 or 14 point; and in a retail advertisement, *merchandising details* might be set in 10 pt. or italic type.

Legibility has been mentioned as the primary criterion. Other criteria, which by now must sound repetitious, should take into consideration:

1.   The kind of store doing the advertising
2.   The merchandise you are selling

3. The customer for whom you are reaching out
4. The appeal you are using
5. The objective of the advertisement
6. The medium that will carry the advertisement.

Color

Perhaps a special area should be devoted to use of color. Any good Art Director will be well equipped to prepare advertising for color as we know it in magazines. But since we are talking about the actual advertising practices of retailers, we should discuss the handling of color in newspapers, which is quite different from the color we are all familiar with in *Vogue*.

ROP color calls for a thoughtful approach right from the beginning of the planning and concept of the advertisement.

The art director is responsible for the concept and the proper preparation of the art. There are a few rules [2] that can be helpful:

1. Bright clear opaque colors and large illustrations give the best results.

2. If transparent watercolors must be used, the colors must be as vivid as possible, and the treatment heavy enough to cover the color of the paper. (Newspaper stock is rarely white; sometimes it is an oatmeal or pale grey color.)

3. Opaque and watercolor treatments are not compatible. Do not use them in the same piece of artwork.

4. Use of overprinting (one color over another) should be avoided, or handled with the utmost care.

5. Reverse type tends to fill up with ink. If the concept calls for light type on a dark background, the type size should completely fill the space, even to being slightly over-sized so that no white outline shows.

6. "Process" color calls for careful register for clear reproduction. Register marks are usually placed in four spots so that the color plates will be set in accurately. Process color is used for the reproduction of half-tone engravings. Thus all photographs must be reproduced by process color.

7. "Spot" color uses line cuts, and, as is true of this kind of art in newspapers, reproduction is easier and "safer."

Additional guidelines will always be supplied by the local newspapers that offer color to their advertisers. Thus, with the responsibility for layout, artwork, and typography his, the Art Director wants to achieve *unity* in his advertising through every element under his control. The readers will recognize this *continuity*, and react favorably to it.

Again, as in the layout, continuity does not imply inflexibility. The artist or photographer who is used for teen-age sportswear may have a style quite different from the artists used for couture clothes. In fact, a store would be highly unlikely to use the same artist, or ask for the same style. In heavy items, such as furniture, appliances, and the like, the style and the artist or photographer used will probably be still another person. But the Art Director will exercise his own good judgment to get the kind of *identification* he wants for his store's advertising.

Color, properly used, adds *excitement* and forcefulness to the advertising. Today the art of the visual must add *dramatic impact* to the selling message.

In closing, then, we can summarize the visual's importance as follows:

1. To capture attention for the advertisement
2. To provide gaze motion to lead the eye the way the advertiser believes it should move.
3. To provide unity, continuity, and identification
4. To add excitement, strength, and dramatic impact.

18

SALES PROMOTION:
THE WHOLE STORE

In a family-owned or small store, the right hand knoweth what the left hand doeth. But how do you achieve the same effect in larger stores? How do you make certain that the budget dress department does not open its new spring line on the same day that the top fashion department slashes all its prices 50%? In a simple question: how do you coordinate the promotional activities of a multi-department store?

The answer lies in the function of sales promotion, a term that should be used to cover *all the efforts* made within a business unit, as a store, from president to parking-lot attendant, first, to promote the store as a desirable place in which to shop and, second, to promote the sales of actual merchandise.

That is a pretty big order. It is a cardinal rule of administration that when something is everybody's job, nobody does anything. Therefore, to be effective, these coordinating functions and powers are generally gathered together in a department called, not unexpectedly, Sales Promotion.

The placement of this department or division has been discussed in the earliest chapters. It is a unit that gathers loose ends together and sets up the overall plan. Therefore, it must be supervisory to Advertising, Publicity, and Display.

While this may seem to some extent to be a duplication of Chapter 5, the importance of this function is such that it merits full presentation in a slightly different way now, at the point where so much of the technique of retail advertising has been absorbed.

All the store has spent on advertising, all that its publicity director has been able to achieve, can be destroyed by surly employees, by slipshod "housekeeping," dirty aisles, and so forth. This is one sense of the term "the whole store."

Another lies, as has been hinted, in the danger of cross-purposes in promotion itself. When a buyer or merchandise manager knows he has a strong current stock, he will want not only advertising, but display in windows and in the department. He may want and deserve a good publicity effort. Special events may be called for. The coordination of all these activities, described for one department of a store, must be further coordinated at least six months ahead of time within the Sales Promotion Division.

When several or all the divisions of a store plan promotions at the same time, the sales promotion director must coordinate and unify the store-wide events. In reality, of course, these various activities have probably first been set up in a coordinated effort by the Sales Promotion Division, and beamed out to the merchandising departments. The needs of one division as against the needs of another, and the reconciliation of competing factions, require a strong, knowledgeable, and respected sales promotion director. The Sales Promotion Division as a whole must hold the confidence of top management (president, board of directors) as well as of the merchandise managers, and of the executives and personnel in its own bailiwick, *i.e.*, Advertising, Publicity, Special Events, and Display.

Very much the same function, responsibilities, and attributes apply to the Shopping Center Promotional Office, often referred to as a Central Public Relations office. Here they have truly competitive stores and shop owners, each needing to add to his own individual promotional plans, the influence and power of the total shopping center promotion.

The specific objective of shopping center promotion is to create traffic, to bring people to the center. The individual retailer must take it from there. It is his own responsibility to bring customers

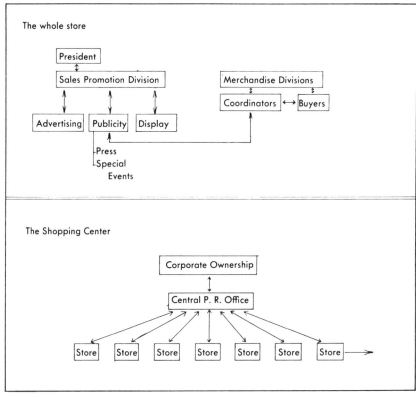

FIG. 26 INPUT/OUTPUT LINES FOR EXCHANGING INFORMATION

off the malls and into *his* store, and from that point, to create sales.

Here, then, the Shopping Center Promotion Office is in a different position from that of a store's Sales Promotion office (Fig. 26).

This responsibility is a two-way street as is the need for reporting. There must be a constant flow of information and planning, down from the top, spreading out to all decisions (within the store) and all stores (within the shopping center).

On the other hand, there must be full reporting on specific activities. In the store, this would be expected, in fact demanded, from all the supporting service departments.

In a shopping center, there should also be reporting back to the center. Here the word could not be "demanded" but "requested." The stores must be encouraged to cooperate in all center-wide promotions. In addition, interesting and/or successful promotion of the store's own creating, whether a special event or an especially good "pull" for an advertising campaign, should be reported to the central promotional office (See Fig. 27).

The means of communication must be some written form. Most stores have forms of many kinds. But the form is only a channel. The actual communication is a lifeline.

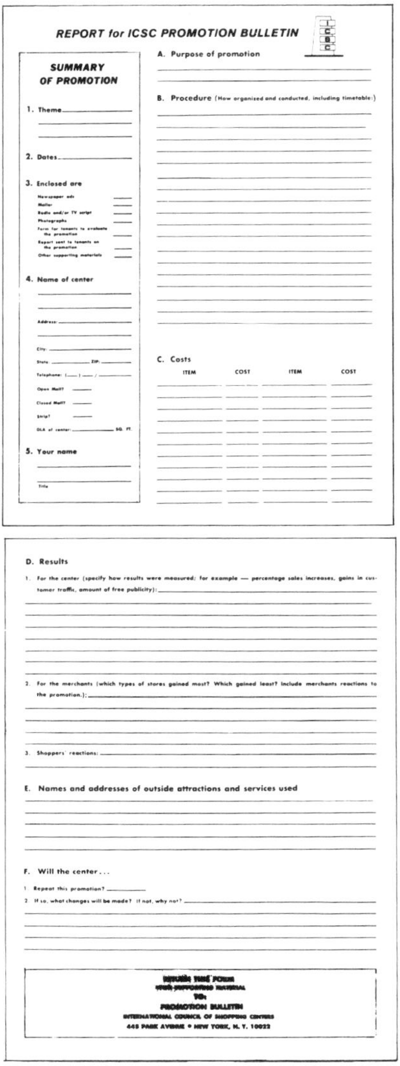

REPORT for ICSC PROMOTION BULLETIN

SUMMARY OF PROMOTION

1. Theme ________
2. Dates ________
3. Enclosed are
   - Newspaper ads ___
   - Mailer ___
   - Radio and/or TV script ___
   - Photographs ___
   - Form for tenants to evaluate the promotion ___
   - Report sent to tenants on the promotion ___
   - Other supporting materials ___
4. Name of center ________
   - Address: ________
   - City: ________
   - State: ________ ZIP: ________
   - Telephone: (___) ___ / ________
   - Open Mall? ___
   - Closed Mall? ___
   - Strip? ___
   - GLA of center: ________ SQ. FT.
5. Your name ________
   - Title

A. Purpose of promotion

B. Procedure (How organized and conducted, including timetable:)

C. Costs

ITEM	COST	ITEM	COST

D. Results

1. For the center (specify how results were measured; for example — percentage sales increases, gains in customer traffic, amount of free publicity): ________
2. For the merchants (which types of stores gained most? Which gained least? Include merchants reactions to the promotion.): ________
3. Shoppers' reactions: ________

E. Names and addresses of outside attractions and services used

F. Will the center . . .

1. Repeat this promotion? ________
2. If so, what changes will be made? If not, why not? ________

RETURN THIS FORM
WITH SUPPORTING MATERIAL
TO:
PROMOTION BULLETIN
INTERNATIONAL COUNCIL OF SHOPPING CENTERS
445 PARK AVENUE • NEW YORK, N. Y. 10022

FIG. 27 AN ICSC REPORT FORM

PART FIVE

PRODUCING
THE ADVERTISEMENT

This section covers a subject that to varying degrees in various stores will always be a major concern of the Advertising Department. The first chapter will cover print advertising. The next will cover radio and television production. In each case, a large part of the job may well be handled by outside shops or studios. Nevertheless, the responsibility rests within the store.

19

PRINT PRODUCTION

In the production of advertisements for newspapers and magazines, the preparation is shared by the Advertising Department of the store and some outside assistance that may vary from store to store.

The Advertising Department's production manager is responsible for the physical translation of the selling message into a newspaper or magazine advertisement. Frequently, he is also the traffic manager.

These two functions, whether or not they are lodged in one person, nevertheless must exist. In the traffic capacity, the person must see that calendar and schedules are observed, that merchandise comes up on time. The "lead" (pronounced like "heed") time is usually eight to ten working days ahead for the large and voluminous Sunday advertising. For simpler daily advertising, six to eight working days ahead provides enough time.

The traffic man also sets dates for the advertising to move along in and out of his own department so that different parts of the whole are ready to be worked on together.

The production man's responsibility is to make certain that the merchandise and the typescript receive the best possible translation into artwork and typeproof, then into the final form that readies the advertisement for newspaper or magazine insertion.

The production man, therefore, works with all members of the department and particularly closely with the art director. He must know the various methods of reproduction and how best to handle line, half-tone, and color material. He must be aware of costs of typography, of engraving, of letter-press printing, of offset. He must be capable of putting out bids and making a wise judgment on quality of workmanship versus reasonable price.

Newspapers

Large city newspapers are generally well equipped to produce copy and artwork and to submit proofs, all at a nominal charge. Smaller newspapers, while always having some kind of facilities

FIG. 28   PRODUCTION PROCEDURE

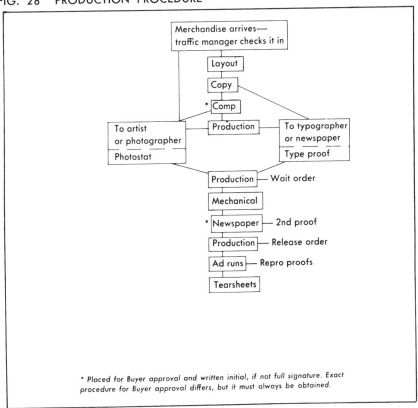

* Placed for Buyer approval and written initial, if not full signature. Exact procedure for Buyer approval differs, but it must always be obtained.

of course, may not have equipment for a special kind or quality of reproduction the store wants.

In these cases (and always for magazine advertising), the production man's job remains the same within his own office, but extends to special suppliers to produce each part of the advertising-to-be. These include, more or less in order of use: photostating, typography, engraving, and (for direct mail) printing. Each of these will be explained.

Now, let us follow a simple single-item advertisement from its inception to its appearance in the newspaper. (Fig. 28.)

Let us suppose, first, that the format has been preplanned, perhaps at a conference earlier in the advertising period, and that the newspaper is large enough to handle setting of the advertisement.

First, when the merchandise arrives with the Buyer's Information Sheet, it is checked by the traffic man against the overall schedule. Then, with a rough layout, maybe even a "pick-up" from another advertisement, it goes to the copywriter for full copy. Always working through the Traffic and Production Department, the merchandise and the copy, now in typescript form, go to the Art Department.

There a "comp," or comprehensive layout, is prepared showing the placement of artwork, copy and logotype. The Art Director at this point prepares the copy for type style and size. The shape of the copy block is also stipulated or marked by the art director at at the same time (Fig. 29). He may call for any of the following in various combinations.

1. "Set solid." This means that the type is to be set in a solid block, i.e., with no space between the lines, or set with the insertion of thin slivers of metal, called "leads," between the lines of type.

2. "Set 3 even lines." The typographer is to set a block of copy with straight margins but in any width that will give three even lines.

3. "Flush left" or "Flush right." This instructs the typographer to straighten up the indicated sides only. "Flush left" means the left margin is straight, and vice versa. In this case, the art director will include a little layout just for the typographer, to show how he envisions the type setting.

4. "Set to pattern" or "Set to layout" usually means that uneven lines of type are to follow an attached layout exactly. In this case, usually neither the left nor the right margins are straight.

In any case, the typescript is sent to the typographer or newspaper to set in type. When a newspaper returns the copy now set in type, this serves as a first proof.

FIG. 29   EXAMPLES OF WAYS TO SET TYPE

1. All are 12' wide. Choose from 27 colors like seamist green, cactus green, cloud white, avocado, imperial ruby, dynasty blue, champagne satin, rice, red, El Greco bronze, more. Not all colors in all qualities . . . limited quantities.

2. **From our own workrooms in pale to darkest tones.**

Low priced in our MAY FUR SALE. Capes from

$195., Jackets from $395., Coats from $1200.

3. # BLAZER

Bold, assertive lapels, broad pocket flaps, jauntily, youthful lines endow this exacting Blazer with almost reckless charm. Faultlessly tailored in Cardin's de luxe edition in navy, forest & burgundy. $125

A graceful desk staunchly crafted, well scaled for limited space, charming and useful in many decorative plans. It has a drop lid concealing a writing area and compartments, plus four lower drawers—these and the lid lock. It measures 40" high, 27" wide. See it now among the many heart-warming discoveries in our Country Living collection.

4. For a focal point in limited space, take a love seat . . . for versatility, a chair pair . . . or splurge on a complete trio! Choose French-inspired curved leg styling, or Italian fluted styling . . . and frames dramatized with large scale caning. richly finished in a warm antiqued fruitwood tone on hardwood. All are in crushed velvet of rayon and cotton—your choice of champagne or gold.

At the same time, ideally, the Art Director has ordered (again through the Production Department) a photograph or illustration of the merchandise.

This, when completed, returns to the Advertising Department. Generally, the artwork is done over-sized. This is desirable for sharpness of reproduction when the art is reduced, and for ease of retouching, if that is necessary. Therefore, when the artwork comes back, it is sent out for photostats to the size wanted by the Art Director, although "stats" are used even if designated "ss" or same size. This is done so that the actual piece of artwork is handled as little as possible.

Somewhere, differing from store to store, buyer approval is sought. Any changes at this stage are minimal, yet the buyer can see what the art and copy look like. Certainly buyer approval or comment on the typed copy would be even more economical, because to change copy on the typewriter costs nothing.

At any stage, buyer approval or correction must be very thorough in regard to merchandise details; buyer comments on the copy approach are not so well received. They must be weighed before any changes are made. These are usually a matter for decision by the Advertising Manager.

To return to the "path of production": when the "stat" and the type are both back in the department, the Art Department proceeds to prepare a "mechanical" or "paste-up." This is an exactly measured replica of the size of the space the advertising will occupy. On it everything is meticulously laid in place including the type-proof of the copy, the photostat of the artwork, the store signature, and miscellaneous information. Here is another point at which buyer approval may be obtained, although it is certainly not recommended at every step. Each store should make its own rules.

The mechanical is then sent to the newspaper or the engraver (for specially designed layouts). The newspaper makes its own plate, called a *stereotype*, and sends a copy back, which represents a second proof. This is usually handled overnight.

The engraver takes longer. Let us remember that he is generally called in, in newspaper work, only for a more complicated or more delicate job.

At this point, careful final approval must be given. Although we have mentioned the buyer, it is absolutely necessary that each member of the Advertising Department involved in a given advertisement be called upon to read and re-read copy, to scrutinize the artwork and to check the proof.

All approvals at all stages must bear the initials of the reviewer; all merchandise advertisements must bear the approval initials of the designated buyer. Advertising personnel have lost their jobs where mistakes were made and *no buyer initials* were found on the proofs. Department approval is important; *buyer approval is a "must."* Do not take telephone shortcuts. They are not valid.

At this juncture, the production man, who has heretofore been working with the newspaper on a "Wait Order," sends the final proof back with a "Release Order" or "Insert Order." It is only upon receipt of the Release or Insert Order that a publication has the legal right to print the advertisement. Prior to that, there was just the holding of space.

Needless to say, the Traffic and Production Department must live by deadlines. Once in the lifetime of a store (and that is once too much) a store misses its deadline. In that dire case, and

Proof of Advertisement

This AD is scheduled to appear IN THIS PAPER		For Dept. Mgr's O.K.	Is this merchandise also at
News Tribune	Times	In signing this proof I certify to the absolute truthfulness of EVERY WORD in this advertisement, and that the merchandise is now in the store and will be price-marked and ready for sale on:	☐
Post	Journal		☐
Herald			☐
Circular	Direct Mail		Do you want to take mail & phone orders on this merchandise? ☐
ON THIS DAY			
Sunday	Wednesday	Dept. Mgr's Signature	Dept. Managers are held responsible for all misstatements appearing in advertisements which they have signed as correct.
Monday	Thursday	Asst. Dept. Mgr's Signature	
Tuesday	Friday		

(FOR INFORMATION ONLY: Remainder of sheet extends 16 inches -- Advertising Department pastes on Proof of Ad.)

ILLUSTRATION 33   Proof of an Ad

you may have seen this once or never, there will be a block of white space with the legend: "Space reserved for ABC Company." That is all, but it is enough to tell all professionals what has happened.

As a final step, the production man receives "repro" proofs in some pre-arranged number. These are distributed to key people in the Advertising Department and the Sales Promotion Department, to store executives, and to the merchandise manager and buyer concerned (Ill. 33).

Until the publication of the newspaper (usually the next day), this is the only notice to those interested of what is running in the next day's paper.

The Telephone Order Board, the Mail Order Department, and the selling department personnel must all have copies at once.

Finally, on the day of issue, the newspaper sends on enough copies for distribution. The Production Department tears out the whole page on which each advertisement appears (even if the advertisement itself took only a small fraction of the page). These pages are called, almost obviously, "tearsheets." They have been referred to before as the only legal proof of performance for obtaining cooperative money from the manufacturer or supplier.

The tearsheet, too, is kept as a store record, in huge scrapbooks that are a part of every Advertising Department. Most modern stores attach a form indicating the ad facts, and some selling facts as well, to serve as a measure of the success of a specific advertisement.

Magazines

The sequence of steps for more complicated, finer quality work, always used for magazine plates, needs some review (Fig. 30). The steps are explained in the chart, and coupled with the discussion on newspaper production, should not need further explanation.

The production concerns itself basically (as previously discussed) with a line cut or a half-tone. In addition, in magazine advertising, there is the real possibility of using full color.

Some magazines use the offset process which eliminates some

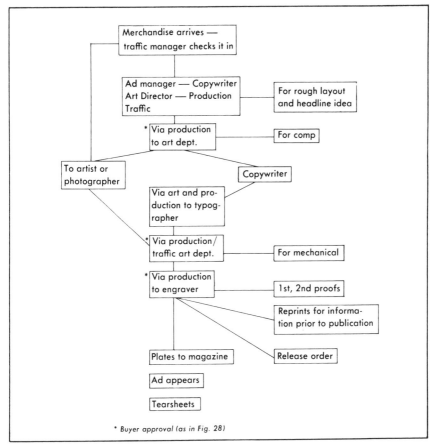

FIG. 31 PRODUCTION OF AN ADVERTISEMENT FOR MAGAZINES

of the step-by-step process necessary in preparing for letterpress reproduction. Printing, then, is done by three processes, mainly:

1. *Letterpress* is like printing with a rubber stamp. Whatever is to be printed is on a raised surface which, after inking, touches the paper to produce a printed image. Sometimes, the type is used directly as it was set; for long runs, duplicates or *plates*, of a longer wearing metal are preferred. Letterpress is the oldest printing method.

2. *Offset.* A metal sheet, coated with a light-sensitive emul-

sion, is exposed to the negative of what is to be printed (black type on white becomes transparent type on a black ground). Areas hit by light—*i.e.,* type or illustration—are activated to accept oily substances and are no longer water-soluble. The sheet is then washed and the non-activated non-printing areas slough off. For printing, the plate, as it is now called, is mounted on a cylinder; simultaneously, it is moistened with water and inked with greasy printing ink. The inked printed areas transfer onto another cylinder, made of rubber, which touches the paper. The printed image is *offset* onto the rubber intermediary to lengthen plate life and to save time just before printing in *make-ready,* or preparation.

3.   *Gravure* is really the opposite of letterpress. Here, plates must be photoengraved, and the printed areas are tiny recessed wells. The plates mounted on cylinders dip into an ink bath; a *doctor blade* wipes excess ink (much thinner than offset inks) and only the ink remaining on the recessed areas touches the paper to print. This method is often used for large printings of many catalogs.

Direct Mail

The production of direct-mail pieces in a retail store cannot be charted, nor need it be. It must be remembered that, under this heading, the store can be sending out a one-pager flyer, a postcard, or a multi-paged Spring Fashion or White Sale catalog. Nevertheless, there are several considerations that can be mentioned here:

1.   This is, indeed, a job that is wholly the responsibility of the Traffic and Production Department (and all the other departments) of Advertising. The material is prepared in the house (with the rarest exceptions), layout is completed, artwork is ordered, and the production done by the store.

2.   It is wise to work with a "dummy." This is first a scaled-down, later an actual size set of sheets of blank paper folded the way the final mailing piece will appear, on which the Advertising Manager, or the copy chief and certainly the Art Director can "rough out" copy and art for the final work.

3.   Every job is different, and once a dummy is laid out, the production man can get bids on the printing. If offset is used, no engravings are necessary. If letterpress is the method of printing, engravings must be figured on.

4.   A knowledge of how the printer will work can help keep costs down. Keep consulting both the engraver and printer, especially the latter, at early stages of the job, and expensive corrections will be eliminated later on.

5.   If color is to be used, it need not be used throughout. It should be used on a layout and may encompass four pages, and will be distributed throughout the booklet as it is stapled or bound. Again, you must know how the booklet will be printed. Later on, you can tell the printer how you want it set up to save your store money.

6.   Printing two sides is generally expensive. It is sometimes cheaper to add a page or two than to look for printing front and back.

7.   Although much more can be said, one last word: get approvals and corrections at the very earliest stages. "Author's alterations" or "AA's" at a later stage are costly.

FIG. 31   ARTWORK WITH A REGISTERED OVERLAY (REGISTERED WITH REGISTER MARKS)

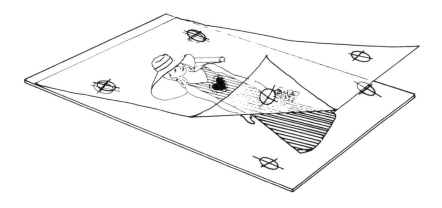

Color

Perhaps some time, however limited, should be given to a discussion of what we mean by the four-color process: In print, as in the paints with which you dabbled in 1st grade, there are three colors (red, blue, and yellow) and there is black. All the subtlest coloring you can detect in a *House and Garden* or *Harper's Bazaar* advertisement is achieved by the use of these four colors. Oranges, greens, purples, pinks—all of them are based on the colors cited. To get the effect in print, color separations are called for; that is, the designation of a yellow plate, a red plate, a blue one, and finally the black added. The *register* must be exact. This means that when the plate is successively printed with the different color inks, the results will appear, as they probably generally have to you, as a perfect whole. Yet, each of us has seen the blurred, multiple edges of a color page, whether an advertisement or a feature. Where such blurring occurs, the register was *not* true. Register marks are shown in Fig. 32 and should be near the four corners of any material prepared for color work.

20

RADIO AND
TELEVISION PRODUCTION

Back in Chapter 16, where we discussed the writing of radio and television commercials perhaps so much had to be said about broadcast production that very little more needs to be added here. Yet, it would be wrong to assume all has been said.

Retailers who use radio and television recognize that this calls for a different set of production skills from those of print. In some large stores, the Advertising Departments have such departments to handle radio and television. But one way or another, any retail advertising personnel ought to know what is involved in such production.

Radio calls for a script certainly, and additionally sound effects and music may be added. After top-level decisions are made on music and sound effects, and script has been written, the next step is a studio to record them. In more costly productions, it may be that an arranger has prepared the music.

In any case, a studio must be rented. The musicians and the announcer come together and record. Sometimes this is done simultaneously, sometimes one after another. The studio engineer and the store representative sit in the control room. "Takes" are recorded until an adequate number of satisfactory takes are on the tape. The studio engineer perfects the mix. The tape (with all the takes) is then listened to and the best recording chosen. This is then put on a master tape with prints taken off for any stations on the media schedule (two to a station).

In smaller cities, where a small schedule or a single station is involved, this local radio station may serve as the studio where all this takes place. Many stations have these facilities. Charges are made to the retailer for production. Sometimes the store can work out a deal with the station that can bring production costs way down.

In *television* production, since sound is ideally recorded first, the start is not dissimilar to that for radio. Thereafter, depending upon the budget, if action is needed, you will need actors, a camera (either for film or increasingly for videotape), lighting, and direction.

A recent study has been devoted to low-cost production to encourage the use of local television for local advertisers.[1] In addition to proving that TV production can be kept at a low cost, it is proving how successful these low-budget commercials are in achieving desired results.

"Ganging up" commercials can keep costs down. That phrase means preparing the merchandise and all the ingredients of a commercial and producing many at a time. A large store in Michigan produced attractive low-budget work by taking two models, a cameraman, and a director to five or six European cities. The whole season's advertising was shot on one trip—travel expenses, pay to personnel, and shooting costs coming in at a feasible price.

The number of stores that handle the production of their own commercials is very small indeed. The best way, therefore, is to call on a studio to submit bids. This can be done for a season or two until you have "shaken down" their qualifications. Then you can move forward more confidently.

A store that begins to use television must expect this shakedown period. The determination to *do it* is the most important factor. The whole department can learn much from actually working with a good studio.

In radio or television production, buyer approval must be secured in the earliest stages. It should be obvious that later corrections are not only prohibitively expensive, but at some points they will be *impossible to carry out*. Control by a top-level member of the Advertising Department should be exercised at all times. In broadcast production, it is usual, in fact desirable for the advertising manager to be present at the recording studio and at the filming and taping sessions.

FOOTNOTE

[1] Study undertaken by TvB, Television Bureau of Advertising, Inc., 1 Rockefeller Plaza, New York, N.Y., 10020.

PART SIX

CONCLUSION

In bringing this text to a close, there remain two areas deserving special treatment. In the chapter that follows, research for the retail store, referred to in many of the foregoing pages, will be reviewed and treated as the vital activity it is. Then, increasing in importance even as this text was being prepared, legal and ethical constraints for retail promotion must be taken seriously, and are so treated in the second chapter of this section.

21

RESEARCH FOR RETAIL PROMOTION

Throughout the book, there have been indications and, it is hoped, clear signals given as to the need and appropriate place for research.

Research is, after all, the *search* for choices or for clues to aid in making a decision. In any area, then, where we have indicated decisions were needed, there has been this prior notice that research was also necessary.

The accumulation of data that can then be analyzed and interpreted must lead to an amassing of information that is useful, pertinent, and *current*.

Every step, therefore, must be covered if research is to be worth even its lowest possible cost:

1. The objective of the research must be clear.
2. An educated guess or a hypothesis may be set forth.
3. The techniques of interview and questionnaire, survey and observation, of study in depth must be examined. Whichever are to be used must be clearly defined in advance. A preliminary pilot study may be advisable if the research plan is finally an extensive one. Such a preview saves time, money, and dead-end effort.
4. The research design must be so planned as to yield valid

214

and reliable results. This means that the sampling must be adequate to cover all sub-groups, an important consideration in any consumer research. It also means that repeated inquiries will yield repeated results pretty much similar one to another. A small margin of error (± 1, ± 2) is always permissible and, in fact, expected.

5.   The data when gathered must be tabulated, analyzed, and given an interpretation according to the findings (not according to some preconceived notion).

6.   The total study must be presented cogently, attractively, and in person. Then the study, fully written up, should be left in the hands of the executive for his later full review.

Research that is delivered by messenger will lie on the executive's desk until it dies of dust-inhalation. Several writers in this subject have pointed out sadly that often mediocre research presented in a lively, personal way with dynamic visuals receives better reception than a fine study coldly sent on in written form alone.

Research for the Store

The Promotion Division as well as store management needs to know everything it can about many elements:

1.   The community the store serves
2.   The store—its present status and future plans
3.   The customer—both present and potential
4.   The merchandise to be promoted
5.   The kind of promotion to use
6.   The media available
7.   The appeals that will work best
8.   Measuring results.

If this sounds familiar, all the better. It has been mentioned in chapter after chapter of this text. The "why" has been explained in the context of each area. In this section, an attempt will be made to discuss sources of this important information and some methods of procedure.

The community can yield its own vital statistics. Depending upon the size of the area and its component parts, this can be a simple or a complicated task. Today's shopping world of huge shopping centers and malls coupled with rapid transportation means that the community of a store may be as diverse as a small town of 6,000 or a giant area of half a million. It may encompass one city or a marketing area of several cities and many suburbs.

Whichever is the case for your store, the governing unit (village, city, etc.) has statistics about itself that can help you gauge the demographics of your area and give you facts you need to know.

The special needs of your community may be obvious. For example, if yours is a store in Gary, Indiana, you know that a large segment of your population derives its income from steel mills. A volume store in that city must get immediate clues about the community and, by extension, about the potential consumer and the kind of merchandise it ought to carry.

The profile of your community might be infinitely complex, as would be the case for a store in the Ala Moana Shopping Center in Honolulu. Here there is not only a diversity of industry, but there is also a diversity of backgrounds, evidenced by the mixture of races and cultures. There is also the variance of life style from that of the *kamaaina* to the *haole* [1] to this morning's tourist.

A seaport, an inland city, a historical site or a tourist attraction, a resort city—each of these presents different situations through its own different character. The store will find itself in a stronger merchandising position as it understands its own locale.

Statistics of all demographic elements are available, not only at the local level but from the state and federal labor departments, to help amass the data that may be needed for a complex understanding of the total consumer the store serves.

The *store* itself, insofar as we can separate it from its merchandise and its customers (and this is the *only* time we should make this distinction), can yield interesting and valuable data.

Basically, we ought to ask where it has been, where it is now, and where it is going. In other words, its history, its current standing, and its future plans are valid areas of research.

The history of the store, if it is anything more than five or so years old, the kind of store it started out to be, can contribute to its promotional plans today. The path the store took to its present position and a close review of that position are important. Attitude and awareness studies are well worth conducting.

The management and personnel of the store itself must certainly be among the first groups interviewed or surveyed. How do the employees see their store? Their opinions and attitudes on every score are pertinent to plans for the way the store will present (promote) itself.

Awareness studies seem almost unnecessary if we talk of a Marshall Field, a Macy's, Sears, and the like. Yet, "awareness" is not just asking, "Do you know that Macy's is there?"

The studies must be refined to yield information as to how much is known about the store, its reputation, what it stands for, and so forth.

Moreover, it is a truism that the vast majority of stores is not made up of huge enterprises. The middle- and small-sized stores can make good use of such studies and need them. Among the people of the neighborhood for even the smallest *modern* store, it would be fruitful to get an idea of what the residents are aware of in regard to the store, what it carries, the kind of service it provides, what they believe it stands for.

To this point, the research may well be conducted at the corporate or top-management level. Frequently, however, a member of the Sales Promotion Division will be given the responsibility for these corporate studies, as well as for those described further on that have to do with promotion.

Very close to this kind of research and really almost like an image, a mirror reflection, is another area of research.

The customer, both present and potential, is a rich lode of information. Here not only the soft or awareness-and-attitude surveys are in order, but the hard, statistical, number-counting studies are equally appropriate.

Where a store has charge accounts or keeps other name-and-address records of customers, it should institute a periodical review of customer purchases. This requires an analysis of the accounts themselves, frequency of visits to the store, departments which made the sales, and dollar-size of such sales.

Non-customers who may well be thought of by the store as prospective customers can be the subject of research by questionnaires, through telephone calls, mailings, or personal interview.

For the investigation of the charge-account customer, the Direct Mail Department within the Advertising Department has easy access to these records and can handle all customer accounts.

The merchandise, both as the total stock of the store and as selections for promotion, should have the closest scrutiny. The merchandise as a whole must, obviously, be what the store's customers want. Analysis can be made of the records that each department keeps of the kinds and amounts of stock sold. A store must know, both in number of units sold and dollar-volume, what its customers are buying. This kind of research is preeminently the responsibility of the general merchandising manager.

Among several new data-gathering electronic devices, Pitney Bowes-Alpex's SPICE has been mentioned (Ch. 8). The promotion department can make good use of the merchandising-flow data provided in instant read-outs by the unit. As more retailers use some version of this kind of computerization, they will gain facility in making its information "work" for the promotion as well as the selling departments of the store.

From these basic records, the merchandise emerges, but only in a general sense. It is the buyer's nose for what is news, coupled with research on what's been selling, that dictates the right merchandise to promote. That there is instinct, the educated guess, or whatever it is called, cannot be gainsaid by those who have seen it work. But actually the top-notch buyer knows how to use it all and, as he has spent his open-to-buy money wisely, he will surely expend his promotional money just as wisely with the right selection of merchandise to promote.

Research for Promotion

Closely on the heels of the last paragraph must come the review that the sales promotion head and the advertising director give to the merchandise that is submitted for promotion. They, too, hold their jobs by reason of an all-around, well-seasoned merchandising know-how, in addition to their talents in their own fields.

In the planning stage, they have made use of all the foregoing research to decide on *the kind of promotion* to use, or what "mix" will serve best.

Although little has been said here about Display (since it is a separate department from Advertising, yet under Sales Promotion), this promotional activity must take its place with Advertising and to a different extent, Publicity, as a strong contender for the promotion of any given merchandise or department.

Stores that are meticulous in their record-keeping have figures to show how window display used alone pulls for given merchandise, what results advertising alone gets, and how the two working together will do. Decisions are made on these factors, among others.

Merchandising departments have the figures, and the Sales Promotion Division has the figures for each aspect of the promotional effort. The merchandise manager, as has been noted much earlier, will have the results of this kind of research for the earliest discussion of plans with the Sales Promotion Division and Advertising Department, and Display Department.

Stores that plan store-wide promotions have careful figures to indicate their success or failure to a precise degree. With a promotion of this kind running over a quarter of a million dollars, as some do, with the army of personnel that must be involved, with the logistics of travel for buying trips and so forth, one can believe that careful dollar-volume charts are evolved, among many other statistics.

Tie-ins are analyzed. One store was persuaded to review its cooperative dollars that it had, year after year, put into Christmas catalogs for direct mail. Three years ago, it took all the available money and put it into a series of television commercials, with a Christmas theme. The results were so satisfactory that this store continued the practice the following year with even more support, and in 1974 will further increase the Christmas TV budget. All the moves were thoroughly investigated, with unit sales and dollar-volume analyses. Customer-attitude surveys were instituted and checked after each of the series.

The media, themselves, supply measurements of their own reach and effectiveness. It remains for the Advertising Department to evaluate them in terms of the store's own needs.

The appeals used in individual pieces of copy, while certainly not the subject of research for each job, are, over a long-range period, subject to careful study. To explain this, there is a real change in the appeal that the high-priced fashion leadership store can use in its promotion from what it used five years ago. Too many sales are lost to the benefit of little stores around the corner who cut the price as they cut out the labels.

Quality and workmanship are not the drawing cards they once were. One such store has said flatly that their customers, who can afford it and to whom they used to sell a $600 dress, now want six $100 dresses or four at $150. Drama, fast changes, impact—these may be today's appeal to those whose mothers, at the very same store, turned the dress inside out to see how the seams were finished.

At the same time, no one in the middle- or low-income class will settle for the "good grey bombazine" (whatever that was) of the early 1900's. Price has to be an object, of course, but even in an advertisement for what used to be called a housedress, you have first to change the name to "patio dress," then show it has fashion appeal, and then, finally, stress its price at $6.99. Then you have appeal in your advertising copy.

Measuring Results

In retailing more often than in any other level of business, the measurement of a promotion and more specifically of an advertisement can be shown in units sold and dollars rung up on the cash register. Where the objective of the advertisement has clearly been sales, this is a valid criterion of success. Units and dollars can be tabulated and a guide for the future is set up.

But, as we indicated in a very early chapter, even in retail stores many other goals are sought when advertising and promotion are set in motion. Just a bare few include: traffic-building, promoting a favorable opinion of the store, instilling confidence in and reliance on the store, building toward interest at a later date, and so on. A store may want to promote or maintain its image as a part of a community and may advertise public events. The possibilities are far wider than those listed here.

To measure the success of this advertising, it will do no good to check the columns of unit sales or check the cash register. The goals were long term, but measurement can be immediate. Once again, a specific awareness study, observation of traffic, of attendance at an event, a before-and-after attitude study will yield solid information.

The important fact here is that the knowledgeable advertising management *does* measure. This all adds up to the necessity for research to become a way of life. It is not a formal exercise to be put away and brought out again once or twice a year. It is a daily accompaniment to modern advertising.

Presenting Formal Research

Despite our insistence on the on-going nature of research even in the most informal way, occasions will arise when a piece of formal research is undertaken, completed, and is to be presented. Some word here about how to present research may prove helpful.

A formal presentation should be made orally and visually, and must be accompanied by the written presentation with usable, easily handled charts. One authority [2] adds a third phase, that of question and answer.

A mass of data thrown together is not research nor, generally, is interpreted data, or information without recommendation. A good presentation will propose a course of preferred action (the primary recommendation) together with alternate roads to take. The risks involved in each, especially for the alternatives, should be explained.

The format of the written report will generally follow this pattern:

1. A title page
2. A summary of findings and recommendation
3. The report with an introduction and a logical development
4. The conclusion elaborating on the summary with supporting data
5. A section of appendix to hold all the material used in gathering the information: questionnaires, motivational research, interviews, bibliography, tabulations
6. Charts and tables incorporated into the body of the report where they seem most appropriate. They should be page size wherever possible.

The oral presentation includes a forceful recital of the summary, with large, easily visible graphs, charts, and tables (if called for). Film strips, slides, color work, and color overlay can help clarify the material.

However handled, it is important to understand that the more knowledge management has about its environment, the better the promotion, the better the results, and the better the annual report of net profit.

FOOTNOTES

[1] Kamaaina—an old timer; haole—the white newcomers.
[2] Myron S. Heidingsfield and Frank H. Eby, Jr., *Marketing and Business Research*, Ch. 15, Holt, Rinehart and Winston, New York, 1962.

22

LEGAL AND ETHICAL
CONSIDERATIONS

The last section of this book was planned from the very beginning, as could be expected. Yet, in the time that has elapsed from planning to this point, it became more and more apparent that the store that stays in business will be the store that keeps itself thoroughly aware of what the consumer wants and expects to find. The store that grows will be the store, as well, that keeps itself abreast of its community's welfare and fosters that well-being. Retailers who expect to weather the tight business conditions must take warning that the consumer will not be fooled. The consumer today looks for full and fair disclosure before making any purchase.

The community will, in turn, support the kind of retailer who helps the positive forces of improvement in the area.

These strong attitudes are being proclaimed through articles in all media, through consumer outcry and the growth of consumer groups, and through actual laws and ordinances passed by federal, state, and local governing bodies.

On the whole, retail advertising has a better reputation than its national counterpart in the realm of honesty. Believability must rest on an honest statement of facts. Leading retail department, specialty, and chain stores can, we think, take some level of pride in a good track record.

Other stores, principally those in "one-line" businesses (of the kind that dot the roads leading into some cities from some airports), must begin to take a hard look at themselves and their flag-fluttering promotions.

Among some of the most-often-voiced consumer complaints are: inadequate stocks of merchandise on advertised items, promotional promises that evidently cannot be kept in the store itself; low prices that apply to a few pieces, with the excuse, "we ran out;" shabby merchandise; fragile toys that were never meant for toddler-handling; exaggeration in artwork, flamboyant copy statements. At some time and in some places, we must face up to it: every one of these complaints is justified.

Guarantees ought to mean what they say, and ought to say it simply and in readable type size. Too many stores additionally hide behind the manufacturers' guarantee (which, in turn, if it means anything at all, entails expensive packing and shipping). Stores that expect to be in business ten years from now may very well have to take over equipment and appliance guarantees. If this is not feasible, then the store should undertake to screen unrealistic guarantees, and undertake to demand bona fide promises and guarantees from the manufacturer for the consumer.

There is a tendency that we must all admit for some proponents of consumerism to go too far, in the apparent, but slightly foolish, "protection" of the consumer. You cannot picket the sale of a vegetable knife because a four-year old might very well use it and cut himself. In some instances cited before government bodies, extreme consumerists have suggested very similar and equally ridiculous "safeguards".

There can be more investigation by the retail store, however, on the dyes and chemicals used, on the possibility of fire-retardant clothing, and so on.

With this care must go advertising controls.

The Comparison Shopping Office which exists in most stores is one such control. These stores require an approval from the Comparison Shopping Office before an advertisement can be released. The office can at least certify that claims of special prices, of special features, sometimes of exclusivity, are true.

The Advertising Department must police itself. It must instill in

ILLUSTRATION 34   On Its 50th Birthday, the N.Y. Better Business Bureau Stresses Its Role in Consumerism

its copywriters a willingness to probe to get at *the kernel of promotable truth* in every piece of merchandise presented to the public.

It can encourage the art department to illustrate what is there, what it sees, not what it would like to see—in a kitchen stove, a dress, or a toy.

Media, too, exercise control and will reject an objectionable or exaggerated claim. A publication or a station can demand proof or refuse to print or air a given advertisement or commercial.

Standards of taste, too, often come under consideration. This is so subjective a matter, however, with such diversity within different regions of this large country, with different levels of acceptance by people of different life styles, that this matter had best be left to the discretion and judgment of each store's Advertising Department. It must, however, be given thought, and generally the taste of the community should provide some clue to what will be accepted by your store's customers.

The Better Business Bureau is exercising increasing power today (Ill. 34), impelled by the same impact as are the stores themselves—a more aware, better educated, more articulate public.

It would be foolhardy to try to enumerate, in a book on advertising, any body of laws or ordinances that exist to control promotion. There are federal laws that apply to every hamlet and every state in the country. But there are also hundreds of state, city, and village statutes that are equally binding wherever they may be.

It would be important for the advertising director to have legal counsel for the store brief him and his staff on whatever laws control that area and that kind of store. Repeated briefing at (at least) yearly intervals would be helpful and, in the end, protective to the store.

Perhaps one last word will suffice. We are all consumers, whether we "sweep out" a store, direct its advertising, or work at a corner garage. Those of us in advertising ought to keep firmly in mind what we ourselves look for in an advertisement in an area different from our own. We ought to apply our own demands to our store's promotion. It sounds simple. It is simple . . . and for once, not new.

APPENDIX

BIBLIOGRAPHY

American Photoengravers Association, *The Fundamentals of Photo-engraving*, Chicago, Illinois, 1966.

Barban and Sandage, *Readings in Advertising and Promotion Strategy*, "Keep Listening to that Wee, Small Voice" by Leo Burnett, pg. 153-162.

Russell H. Colley, *Defining Advertising Goals*. Association of National Advertisers, 1961.

Kenneth A. Collins, *Successful Store Advertising*. Fairchild Publications, New York, 1959.

James Craig, *Designing With Type*, Watson-Guptil Publications, New York, 1971.

William R. Davidson and Alton F. Doody, *Retailing Management*, 3rd ed., The Ronald Press Company, New York, 1966.

Charles M. Edwards, Jr. and Russel A. Brown, *Retail Advertising and Sales Promotion*, 3rd ed., Prentice-Hall, Inc., Englewood Cliffs, N.J., 1965.

Albert Wesley Frey and Jean C. Halterman, *Advertising*, 4th ed., The Ronald Press Company, N.Y., 1970.

Irvin Graham, *Encyclopedia of Advertising*, 2nd ed., Fairchild Publications, Inc., New York, 1969.

228

McLuhan, Marshall, *Understanding Media: The Extension of Man,* McGraw-Hill Book Company, New York, 1964 (also Signet Books).

Milton, Shirley, *Advertising Copywriting,* Oceana Publications, Dobbs Ferry, New York, 1969.

Myron S. Heidingsfield and Frank H. Eby, Jr., *Marketing and Business Research,* Holt, Rinehart, and Winston, New York, 1962.

Thomas S. Robertson, *Consumer Behavior,* Scott, Foreman and Company, Illinois, 1970.

RESEARCH QUESTIONNAIRE

Editor's Note: The questionnaire which appears below was used by the author to obtain the information which appears throughout the book from various stores around the United States.

A. GENERAL INFORMATION:
    1. City _____ 2. Population _____
    3. Store Name _____ 4. Type _____
    5. Sales Volume $_____
    Executive Responding (should be Adv. Mgr. or Director ideally):
    6. Title _____ 7. Name _____

B. ORGANIZATION OF THE ADVERTISING DEPARTMENT:
    1. Size of Department _____
    Number of people whose time is devoted to store's advertising:
    2a. Full-time _____ 2b. Part-time _____
    What services do they perform:
    3a. Planning _____ 3b. Copywriting _____ 3c. Art Direction _____
    3d. Artwork _____ 3e. Production _____ 3f. Media Selection _____
    3g. Clerical _____ 3h. Advtsg. Accounting _____ 3i. Other _____
    4. Is an Advertising Agency or Advertising Service used? _____
    5. If answer to #4 was "Yes," proceed with these:
    What services do they perform:
    5a. Planning _____ 5b. Copywriting _____ 5c. Art Direction _____
    5d. Artwork _____ 5e. Production _____ 5f. Media Selection _____
    6. Title of top advertising executive: _____

7. To what officer (title) does this person report? _____

8. Titles of other members of Advertising Department:

_____

_____

_____

9. Does your store have a Sales Promotion Director? _____
   If answer is "Yes," proceed:
   9a. Is the Sales Promotion Director "above" the Advertising Director? _____
   9b. Does the Sales Prom. Dir. report to the Adv. Dir.? _____
   9c. Is the S.P.D. synonymous with the Adv. Dir.? _____

10. What department handles Publicity? 10a. Corporate _____
    10b. Press Publicity _____ 10c. Product Publ. _____
    10d. To whom does the Publicity Dept. or executive report? _____

11a. Does the Advertising Department have any responsibilities in the Display function? _____
     11b. What are these responsibilities or functions? _____

12a. Does the Advertising Department have any responsibilities in the presentation of Fashion Shows? _____
     12b. What are these responsibilities or functions? _____

Is your copywriter(s) expected to write:
   13a. copy for signs and/or posters? _____
   13b. scripts for fashion shows? _____
   13c. releases for publicity? _____

C. PLANNING AND BUDGET:
   1a. Does your store prepare long-range plans? _____
   1b. If so, how far in advance? _____
   2. How far ahead is *departmental* planning done? _____
   3. Does your store have a formula for determining the advertising budget? _____
   4. If possible (or willing), please indicate how the figure is arrived at:
      4a. "Task" Method _____
      4b. Matching (or surpassing) the competitor _____
      4c. Percentage of projected sales volume _____
      4d. If your method is "4c," what is the % _____
      4e. Other _____
      Comments welcome here:

_____

_____

_____

_____

D. MEDIA:
   What is the major medium used for your store advertising:

1.a Newspapers _____ 1b. Magazines _____ 1c. Radio _____
1d. Television _____ 1e. Direct Mail _____ 1f. Other _____
2. If your store does (or expects to do) Radio and/or Television Advertising, does your Advertising Dept. have separate personnel _____ or a sub-department _____ to handle this type of advertising? Comments: _____
3. If so, does this staff include:
   3a. Copywriters _____ 3b. Production Men? _____
   3c. Media Buyer(s) _____ 3d. Other? _____
4. Who of the following is *primarily and finally* responsible for Media Selection:
   4a. Merchandise Manager _____
   4b. Buyer _____
   4c. Advertising Manager _____
   4d. Designated member of the Advtsg. Dept. _____
   4e. (If applicable) Advertising Agency _____
   4f. Other _____

E. BRANCH STORES:
   1. Does your store have branches? _____
   2. If so, how many?
      2a. 1 to 5 _____ 2b. 6 to 10 _____ 2c. 11 to 25 _____
      2d. over 25 _____
   3. Are any of the advertising functions handled directly by the branch _____ or groups of branches _____
   4. If so, what functions are so handled?
      4a. Planning _____ 4b. Copywriting _____ 4c. Artwork _____
      4d. Production _____ 4e. Media Selection _____
   5. Again, if answer to #3 was "yes," where are the branch advertising functions performed—5a. Main store _____ 5b. In branch itself _____
   6. If located in branch store itself, is this because of
      6a. Distance from main store _____
      6b. Administrative decision and policy _____

F. COOPERATIVE ADVERTISING:
   How would you describe your store policy towards Co-op Advertising:
   1a. Encourages ___ 1b. Accepts ___ 1c. Rejects ___ 1d. Other ___
   2. Does your store reserve the right to adapt advertising of this nature to its own format? _____
   3. Do you consider that Co-op Advertising, if *ideally* handled on both sides, is
      3a. Beneficial to the store _____ 3b. Beneficial to the vendor _____
      3c. Nonetheless unacceptable _____
   4. Do you consider that Co-op Advertising, *as it exists* (whether "ideal" or not), is
      4a. Beneficial to the store _____ 4b. Beneficial to the vendor _____
      4c. Unacceptable _____

G. MERCHANDISING vs. PROMOTION
(Should be answered by store head or someone with jurisdiction over advertising and merchandising.) In the following specific advertising functions, in case of a real disagreement, whose decision would prevail:

FUNCTION	MERCHANDISING MANAGER	ADVERTISING MANAGER
1a. Planning		
1b. Budget		
1c. Media Selection		
1d. Seasonal Promotions (headlines, graphics, etc.)		
1e. Advertising copy		
1f. Product Artwork		

H. CONCLUSION:
1. Will you give the author permission to use your store name _____ and to credit the information you've given to the store? _____
2. Will you permit the author to quite any part of your responses? _____
3. Do you want your own name used? _____
4. Should additional questions arise, may we come back to you for your answers and/or comments? _____
5. If pertinent, may the author reprint any of your store's advertising? _____

*   *   *   *   *   *   *   *   *   *

6. In the last quarter of this century, what do you believe will be the greatest service retail advertising can perform for
6a. The Consumer _____

6b. The Retailer _____

7. In the same period, what do you believe will be Retail Advertising's greatest need? _____

*   *   *   *   *   *   *   *   *   *

Your comments will be more than welcome.

INDEX

advertising: "assortment," 127; copy, see copy, definition, 2-7; departmentalized, 127; non-personal factor, 2; "round-up," 127; "single-item," 127

advertising agencies, see agencies

advertising department: art director, 26-7; clerical help, 27; copy department, 25-6; displays, 6; fashion shows, 6, 28; functions, 8-10; manager, 24-5; multi-branched store, 19; organization, 24-33; policing, 225-6; production, see production; publicity, 6; Sales Promotion Division, relation to, 28, 30; shopping centers, 18-9; Special Events, 6, 28; staff, 24-8; traffic, 27, 198

advertising manager, 24-5

advertising research, see research

agate line, 93

agencies, 31-2, 58-9; artwork, 185; institutional advertising, 32; magazine advertising, 87; Special Events, 32; television advertising, 32, 92

American Newspaper Publishers Association, Bureau of Advertising, 15, 81

appliances, advertising of, 13

appropriations, see budgets

art agencies, 185

art director, 26-7; career opportunities, 35; qualifications, 35

artwork, 179-91; agencies, use of, 185; Ben Day screen, 184; classification for reproduction, 184; color, 190-1; costs, 184-5; half-tone art, 184; lettering, 185-6; line drawings, 184; photography versus illustration, 181-4; "process" color, 190; "spot" color, 190; typography, 185-90; wash drawings, 184